The GOLDEN HOUSE on SILVER STREET

I0370816

Light Bright Publications

© 2018 Rosemary McLain

All rights reserved

Published by Light Bright Publications

Cover Design: Dylan Wickstrom, DoubleyouDesign
Interior Design/Editing: AuthorSource

No part of this publication may be reproduced, stored in a retrieval system, or transmitted in any form or by any means—electronic, mechanical, photocopy, recording, or any other—without the prior permission of the author.

ISBN: 978-1-947939-99-8

Printed in the United States of America

TABLE OF CONTENTS

PROLOGUE v

ACKNOWLEDGMENTS xvi

CHAPTER 1: A New Beginning — 1

CHAPTER 2: A Treasured Heritage — 7

CHAPTER 3: Celebrating Her Historical Splendor — 13

CHAPTER 4: Something Is Not Right — 23

CHAPTER 5: A Violent Past — 33

CHAPTER 6: Is This Really Happening? — 49

CHAPTER 7:	Don't Mess With My Family	53
CHAPTER 8:	Experiences of Others	67
CHAPTER 9:	Paranormal Events Intensify	81
CHAPTER 10:	Saying Goodbye	97
Epilogue:	No Better Place to Call Home	105
Historic Photos		113
APPENDIX:	Recorded Property Deeds	121

PROLOGUE

A Word from the Author

In July of 1987, I purchased the property described in this story. My husband Allen and I had been traveling a great deal in an attempt to locate an investment property which we could develop and thus begin anew, somewhere else. We eagerly sought a place where we could find work and happiness, away from the maddening crowds of the city. At the time, we were living in Mesa, Arizona and had recently closed an interior design shop that we had operated for a few years. We had found the constant battle to secure payment for our labors to be so draining as to make it not worth the effort.

At the time of our impending move to New Mexico, Christine (my then twenty-year-old daughter) was working and going to college at night. She chose to remain in Arizona and continue her life there. She had a good head on her shoulders, and I felt that the time was right to let her try her wings. She endured well. She had proven her personal worth to herself and to all who know her. She is a fine, quite wonderful young woman.

John (my then seventeen-year-old son) decided that he would stay with us. He had one more year of high school when we left Phoenix. He graduated from Deming High School in 1988. In August of that year, he chose to enter the United States Coast Guard. I watched him mature and grow with pride in his quiet strength. John married and now has a beautiful wife and two daughters.

Mark, my youngest son (then fifteen-years-old), chose to try to live with his biological father. He wished to stay in the same area to continue high school with his friends. This didn't work out well. In time, Mark chose to come back home and finish his last year of high school in New Mexico, as his brother John had. This did not work out very well due to the series of events that I will relate to you in this book. We eventually moved to Tucson, and he graduated there. Mark then chose to enter the military as well, deciding to serve in the United States Navy. He also married and had three children prior to divorcing his wife. He now lives with a wonderful woman who has given him three additional children and mothers all six with genuine care and love.

In the first couple of years of owning the property, my husband and I worked tirelessly to restore the home to as close to its original state as possible. Through the removal of many layers of wallpaper and other more modern touches that had been added to the home over the years, we began to reveal the home's genuine beauty and uncover a myriad of historical discoveries.

In 1989, the stresses and hardships of dealing with our ordeal had taken their toll on both my husband and me. We decided to divorce and he left New Mexico to begin a new life elsewhere. By that time, he had spent almost one and a half years in the house with me, and he contributed a great deal to her restoration. I was alone in the house until that fall when Mark came home.

Mark's return home was marred by a distinct increase in haunting experiences. I am continually asked about the things that occurred during these years of my life, things experienced by family, my neighbors, friends, renters, acquaintances, and myself. This book is meant to answer some of those persisting questions. Some of these stories are recounted directly by those who lived them firsthand.

When we embarked on our journey to restore and bring recognition to the U.S. Customs House on Silver Street, we had no idea of the inexplicable phenomena that would eventually plague us in this beautiful historical property. Moreover, I had no idea how much I would grow to love and cherish both the home and the entire region.

My family members and I experienced the events detailed in this book personally. There were others who had similar experiences during the time period in which I owned the property, and I have shared their experiences as well. Because of the paranormal nature of these occurrences, as well as the historical significance of the property, I felt that it was important to relate the total of our experiences to you, the reader. The wide spectrum of events that the purchase of this house forced upon me was totally foreign to my belief system. Up until that point in my life, I had no personal experience, either intellectually or emotionally, with spirits, ghosts, or whatever name you would give a supernatural presence; that was until my experiences with our beautiful, historical home. I was now, however, compelled to accept the possibility of paranormal forces as part of my life. It was certainly not an easy journey, but it is one that I felt very strongly that I must share.

My desire is that my story will help any others who walk this way of strange and unsettling occurrences. Know that you are not alone in your experiences. You are not mad. There is another dimension of existence to deal with in this old world—a dimension that lies just under the surface of our comprehension. The story that follows is a valid account of my experiences composed from notes and audio tapes which I recorded at various times during my life in this house.

Many were the times that I questioned my perceptions. Many were the times that I thought I was going quite mad only to have another confirm what I could not accept on my own judgment. Most times, these individuals were unaware of their contribution to my sanity. Just knowing that someone else lived through the same things I was experiencing was comforting beyond words.

PROLOGUE: A Word from the Author

This was a completely new realm of reality for me, one which required extensive mental adjustment and a reorientation of basic concepts by which I had lived my entire life. Enough said. There are many stories between July of 1987 and April of 1994. These are what follow, for your reading enjoyment. For you who have been there, enjoy my tale. For those who have not, read my story and take heed, for you may find yourself faced with a similar inexplicable encounter at some point in your journey on this earth.

A WORD FROM ROSEMARY'S SON

I came across my mother's book while cleaning out her home after her death. I knew that she had been working on a book covering all of her efforts and experiences while preserving the Golden House but I had never read any of her writing up to that point. As I worked my way through photos and legal papers and the like, I found a box full of rough drafts and revisions, various notes, historic information and a few audio cassettes. I knew that I had to preserve this legacy of hers and get it into a finished form if only just to have it completed. So, I packed up everything and brought it back with me to New Jersey. The box sat for a few months while my siblings and I concluded her personal affairs and I fulfilled the requirements of her last will and testament. Then one day, I felt the nudge to open the box and delve into The Golden House on Silver Street.

As I read through the various dated drafts and revisions, I was amazed at the writing talent that was before me. She was able to paint such a vivid mental picture of this glorious house and the wonderful landscape in which this story is based. She eloquently expressed just how deeply she loved this place and how determined she was to bring *her* back and keep *her* alive for generations of Americans to experience. In addition, my mother's loving perspective and peaceful personality shone through her writing like the sunlight bursting through those old glass windows which wrapped around the house. I knew she was an amazing person with limitless talents but I never knew that writing was one of them.

Reading the drafts also brought to my attention just how significant her achievement was in saving this part of American history. The sheer amount of research and interaction with government agencies to recognize this national treasure and formally preserve it was incredible. The house is now officially called, "The Old Customs House" because of her work. It very easily could have become a parking lot extension for the city public works department. She pushed through several discouraging setbacks and will-crushing nights of paranormal craziness refusing to give up even though she had reached her limit on several occasions. She kept her goal in sight and always looked to the future even when the horizon was darkened by fear and physical and emotional exhaustion. Living across the country, and for a time, across the world, I don't think that I fully grasped the extent of what she was

PROLOGUE: A Word from the Author

enduring. She never let on, to me, just how incredibly challenging and horrifying her days in the house became at times. I know she did this as not to worry me.

So, after sorting through her drafts and listening to her audio recordings, I got to work on retyping and editing her last revision. There were only printed copies and a floppy disk to work from so I labeled a Word document with the title and began at the beginning. She had recorded the audio initially while in the midst of her adventure and then expanded on those recording while writing the text. I transferred the cassettes onto CD to preserve her audio journals. The audio is very difficult to listen to for me. As her child, I know the inflections and tone of her voice and can clearly hear the joy, fear, sorrow, depression, discouragement, excitement, love and hope in her recordings at the various points in her saga. Listening to my mother on these tapes, as she endures some of the most trying times of her life, is an incredibly emotional roller coaster. I often wonder if others who never knew her would feel the same hearing her voice as she details the events of her life in those years. To this day, I do not believe my sister or brother have listened to the tapes.

The work to edit and transfer the written work to a digital form took several months to complete. I took my time and looked at every word, every sentence and every paragraph ensuring proper grammar, spelling, sentence and paragraph structure, spacing, etc..... Along with this, I fact checked the historical information, to the best of my ability from across the country, to make sure that this book was the best that it could be. I owed it to her to do my very best to make this book worthy of her effort. I had to take breaks along the process due to the responsibilities of raising a family and the obligations of a military life. Sometimes it would be a couple of months in between sessions but I never gave up on making her dream a reality.

After I completed the digital draft of the book, I sent copies out to my brother and sister. I had no clue as to where to go next or how to proceed with getting this initial edit into print and publication. My sister came in on the project and became the driving force in moving the work forward. We talked often about our wishes for our mother's work and how to move toward publication. The book sat for many months while we figured out how to proceed. My sister had worked with an editor in Ohio to edit a couple of professional books that she had co-written for her business and suggested we use her to look over the book and do a professional edit on the content. This became the catalyst we needed to relight the engines and move the book forward again. After a few revisions, we had the amazing piece of work which we have now. Thank you Beth Lottig!

After the editing was complete, we went through a few other periods where our efforts stalled out for a few months before picking back up. Mostly this was due to the fact that we simply did not know how to proceed. Did we need an agent? Did we need to send chapters to a publishing house? Self-publish or e-Publish? How to get an agent? How to get a publisher? How to protect her work?

Finally, we decided to self-publish. My sister contacted her editor in Ohio seeking a cover artist and someone to design the text for print. Meanwhile, we created a Facebook page to promote the upcoming book and gain some exposure. I reached out to several paranormal investigation groups in the southwest area to introduce myself and detail the opportunity that the Golden House presents for a hair-raising experience. On October 28th, 2017, one such paranormal group completed an after dark walk through tour and investigation of the house with about 40 other curious members of the community. The ghosties did not disappoint!

So, we are now releasing Rosemary's work to the world in hopes that it may inspire others to seek out this Golden House and learn about the history that is ingrained within the boundary of her walls. See for yourself, the grand architecture and feel the love that filled my mother's heart so full while she was there. Touch the walls and imagine how this house has forged US history through the years. Read her story and ponder what she went through to keep this national treasure alive. Explore the area of southwestern New Mexico and see for yourself why it is called, "The Land of Enchantment."

John Barbieri
Rosemary's Son

A WORD FROM ROSEMARY'S DAUGHTER

The Golden House on Silver Street is a tremendous story that my beautiful mother leaves behind as part of her legacy. When she and her husband, Allen McLain, purchased the home so many years ago, it was perplexing at best as to the impetus behind the purchase. After visiting, I realized everything she hoped it would be, was going to come to fruition with their ownership. Little did she know what they had gotten themselves into.

I honestly can say I had no idea as to the magnitude of the history, beauty or paranormal happenings until I visited the Golden House on Silver Street in person. My mother's countless hours of research, interviews and diligent persistence revealed such a fruitful history and picture of a time long forgotten. Reading her notes for the first time, as I tried to piece together the different thoughts she had, I soon realized this story would serve as a significant part of her life. Having said that, she would not have wanted it to be about her, but more so the house itself. The history, the people, the circumstances they found themselves in; she found total fascination in learning about their stories.

The book truly has been a labor of love from our family to yours. While my mother penned and lived this story, my brothers and I have been heavily vested in ensuring that story is revealed and told. My hope for you the reader, is that the rich history that took place in this house, the people who carefully cared for the property and the legacy of immigration and Customs isn't lost in the paranormal happenings. While key to the story and a significant part of my mother's reason for leaving the home, it truly isn't the only view into this historic landmark. My hope is that you sit back, use your imagination to transport yourself to another era and to experience what life might have been like coming to the United States and experiencing for yourself the Golden House on Silver Street.

With love,

Christine Gannon
Rosemary's Daughter

ACKNOWLEDGMENTS

Rosemary's family would like to thank the following people for their hard work and dedication while assisting in bringing her work into print. Without their help, this book would not be what it has become.

Editor: Beth Lottig, AuthorSource – Beth did a comprehensive edit of the rough draft including arranging chapters, consolidating the content and taking the many different sections of the book to create a flow and readability. She did an outstanding job of organizing the many facets of this book and intuitively placed key elements of the story together to create a very vivid account of our mother's experiences with the Golden House. Beth was also instrumental in structuring the final design and formatting the text as well as incorporating last minute changes and corrections. We believe that she came to truly understand and appreciate our mother's vision and used that insight to mold her writing into a piece of literature that Rosemary would most undoubtedly love.

Cover Art: Dylan Wickstrom, DoubleyouDesign – Dylan worked patiently with us to design the front and back covers of the book. He did a fantastic job of taking our initial ideas and presenting us with several variations while maintaining the underlying theme of the story. He quickly incorporated our suggestions and modification requests, providing us with visual examples of the various fonts and background options. We are very happy with how well the cover elements encompass the essence of her story.

CHAPTER 1

A New Beginning

How could we be so lucky?
It was everything we had hoped for and more.

My journey with the Golden House on Silver Street began in the summer of 1987, another stifling hot July in the southwestern United States. My husband and I had been earnestly searching for an investment property where we could find work and fulfillment away from the hustle and bustle of the crowded city. Our search for a healthier and more rewarding area began in Texas. We visited San Antonio, Austin, Corpus Christi, and numerous points in between, but the humidity of the gulf coast did not agree with my husband. Next, we tried New Mexico. Voila! It seemed like the perfect fit for our family. At the center of the fertile Mesilla Valley and nestled in the flood plain of the

Rio Grande, we discovered the quiet little town of Las Cruces in the southeast corner of the state, not far from the Texas border.

As we explored the area, we found a perfect little complex in the downtown section of Las Cruces. It seemed ideal for our needs. We made an offer, and it was accepted. We soon returned to complete the deal when fate stepped in and said, "Not this one!" The seller was a recently widowed woman who had realized, at the last moment, that she could not part with her home. Too many memories, I suppose. So, with tears in her eyes, she asked for release from the contract. No one could have refused this woman's plea. Our search would continue.

We had some unfortunate car trouble, so we got a late start on our trip home to Mesa, Arizona. With a little more time to kill, we decided to stop and stay the night with a dear friend of ours who lived in Deming, a small town about sixty miles west of Las Cruces. The next morning, she suggested we take a look around her little town for a place. She seemed to be very happy there, so we took her up on the suggestion. *You never know*, I thought to myself.

We toured the town with one of her real estate friends for most of that day and the next. Around midday, we rounded a corner by the local museum and saw a "For Sale" sign in front of the house directly across the street. I immediately was drawn to the sense of old time grandeur it emitted.

"Hey, I'd like to see that one," I said to the realtor.

CHAPTER 1: A New Beginning

"Are you sure?" she replied. "That's a bit more money than the properties we've been looking at."

We decided that we would consider the property despite the higher price tag—there was just something about it that made me want to take a closer look.

When we stepped through the front door, we were absolutely overwhelmed with what we saw. Large windows were everywhere with light—beautiful sunlight!—pouring through the antique glass into every corner of the room. There was no center hall, so every room opened into the next, each one enchanting and inviting with warmth and charm to spare. A grand total of eight full rooms and a few partial rooms melded together to make up the interior of the house. Two full baths were furnished with very large, old claw-foot bathtubs, impeccably flanked by little round sinks. Crystal knobs accented the wooden towel racks. The kitchen and dining area ran almost the full length of the house. At one end of the kitchen were two sets of beautiful old French doors. One set led into the bedroom, and the other led into a small sitting room that contained a large stone fireplace. Outside, a private walled-in courtyard sat directly off that room. Along one wall was a gate that opened into a huge backyard.

It was simply enchanting. With each room we toured, my affection for the home grew. I imagined how beautiful she would be once we were able to restore her to her original glory. We continued our tour as we explored the outdoor grounds.

Our eyes were immediately drawn to the white painted wall comprised of adobe and masonry block that surrounded the entire property like a guardian. In one corner of the yard stood an old stone fireplace. Large, mature trees were everywhere. Directly behind the walled-in yard were twin earthen driveways separated by tall Cypress trees which formed a shaded arch of green. English Ivy grew from around the trunks of these Cypress, over old stumps, along the walls, and spread out upon the earth like a carpet.

At the far end of the drive stood a large double garage just waiting to become our workshop. Included with the property were two small guesthouses located adjacent to the garage, each completely unique.

After the tour, Allen and I looked at each other. We didn't have to say a word. A single spirit flowed between us. How could we be so lucky? It was everything we had hoped for and more. Within an hour, we had signed the papers.

We asked the realtor about the age of the property and were told that it was approximately fifty years old, give or take a few years. We found out later on that it was closer to one hundred and sixty-seven years old, and our research would reveal that the first known records of the house were dated back to 1820.

We experienced many types of delays before we could move into the main house and feel that we were truly there and ready to go.

CHAPTER 1: A New Beginning

Finally, the day came when we were really in our new home. We were ready for our new beginning.

CHAPTER 2

A Treasured Heritage

*The house seemed to glow from within
with an overabundance of delightful stories
from such a vast array of people.*

The next year proved to be a tough one. If you have ever seen the movie titled, "The Money Pit," then you can understand what our first year was like. Not that it ended there, however. Rather, the first year was the period of time that it took for us to realize what we had gotten ourselves into! A constant outpouring of funds was required for restoration, repair, replacement, research, and tender loving care of the home. But it was a sacrifice that I felt was truly worthy, because the home had truly become, at least to me, a living thing of overwhelming beauty and grace. She was a grand ole' dame who had held on through some tough years.

Shortly after we moved in, the U.S. Customs Department showed up at our door. They were wondering if this could possibly be the "Lost Customs House" they had seen referenced in various old ledgers located in the archives in Washington D.C. and El Paso as well as other documents from the area. We confirmed to them that we had been made aware of the customs-related background by the family of the customs collector, Seaman Field, who had bought the house back in 1887. The customs officers explained that the coming year was a bicentennial year for the U.S. Treasury and customs departments and that they would like to include the house in the celebration which was being planned for this occasion. We worked closely with them, and together we researched the history of the house. As a result, it eventually became a part of the National Bicentennial Celebration of the Customs Department in 1989.

During a gala event held on the property, the house and all its grounds were declared a federal, state, and national historic site. First, it was declared a federal historic site, then a state historic site, and finally, on February 20, 1990, it was entered into the National Registry of Historic Places. My efforts and goals were met well beyond my hopes. The experience became a treasure of events that I consider to be an incredible achievement—an achievement to be remembered in times of need for self-assurance of personal value to my country and to my ancestors.

Why was I so driven to restore the property to its former glory and secure its place in history? As a fifth generation American,

CHAPTER 2: A Treasured Heritage

I wanted to honor the memory of the earliest recorded direct descendant of our family tree, Richard Jackson, who arrived in this great land from England in 1572. With all of my hard work and dedication to the task at hand, I feel as though I can say, "Here's my addition to our family's stone soup!"

Love of God and country was a trait imbedded in our family as a basic principal of life. Being in a position to contribute to the better good (in this small but personally significant way), by securing the public recognition and federal acknowledgement of this wonderful piece of our country's history, filled me with such pride. An honor and a privilege of such personal satisfaction, this would remain a permanent part of my legacy to my children. Throughout the trials and immensity of hard work over the years of owning and restoring the home, I had unwavering perseverance toward my goal, just as my ancestors had practiced.

The oldest United States Customs House and port of entry in the great state of New Mexico, and possibly the oldest on our southwestern border (as one Customs official confided in me), was, in my view, well worth my dedication of time and my pursuit of purpose. I committed myself, wholeheartedly, to do the very best I could to save her from loss and to secure her future existence for those who followed. I continuously thought of the Americans who would want to look upon, to touch, and to experience a place in this nation's history where their fellow Americans had settled, planted their feet, and proceeded to build a country.

HISTORICAL DISCOVERIES ABOUND

As we peeled back the layers of years gone by during the restoration process, we discovered that many methods had been used to keep the home going by those who, in the past, had also loved her. The seven layers of wallpaper we removed read like a story detailing each time period in history when remodeling had taken place. We felt like we were archaeologists as we discovered such findings as paneling on top of the wallpaper, windows covered over with boards, and adobe mud and chicken wire throughout the main house and both guest quarters. *What wonderful memories had these old walls borne witness to?* Each layer provided a unique view into the delightfully historic life of the house.

It was truly like a fantastic treasure hunt! A square section of one bathroom floor was removable, revealing a hole—maybe a kind of hiding place or safe for valuables at some point in time. Another large square was cut in the kitchen floor, and yet another secret was revealed. This one led to a set of stairs with an angle of descent that required you to literally go down on your hands and feet, almost sitting down, in order to pass through a dark, narrow passage. It led into a small room that would later be identified as a type of cellar by some of the old timers from the museum across the street. Originally located in the backyard, this room was used as a hiding place by the pioneer family that had once lived there. The narrow hallway and entry steps enabled the man to protect his family by allowing space for only one invader at a time to get into their hiding place—a considerable advantage for him. Whether armed with a musket, knife, or whatever weapon he chose, he could take invaders on one at a time.

The dining area had all glass windows on the side facing the backyard. Sitting there at the table in the afternoon, with the sun gleaming on the green flooring from an era long past and the wood around the French doors giving off a warm glow, one was transported through both time and space. An inner glow developed within your soul. The antique glass in the bay windows at the opposite end of the room bounced the sun's rays off of the green hanging plants and the dried and shriveled red chilies hanging there. My Grandma's rocking chair, with its patchwork pad, seemed to begin rocking with childhood memories filled with the sounds of lullabies and the feel of a lap with loving arms and hands holding me. Oh, those treasured memories. It made me wonder if she could see me then and know how hard I was trying to save this house—this wonderful house where time stood still (or rather rolled back), not only for me but for so many others that stopped by.

The house held special memories for a great many of my guests. They would get that faraway look in their eyes as if they were actually brought back in time to a specific emotional moment in history. "Did you know that I got married in this room fifty years ago?" questioned one guest.

In addition to the many weddings held in the home, there were countless parties and celebrations of all kinds held there. It seemed that May Field, one of the original residents of the home, rented the main room out for weddings and social occasions of all kinds, as it was the biggest place in town. So many people stopped by to share their memories with us during our time in the home. I could imagine delightful affairs with music and dancing, the guests laughing and reveling in the beauty and grandeur of her treasured rooms.

Through the vivid remembrances of my guests, these happy times were revealed to me often. Even when my sons and husband had moved on and there was only me left in the home, they still came to reminisce and to share their special recollections. It was an honor to be a small part of restoring the setting of their treasured memories.

The house seemed to glow from within with an overabundance of delightful stories from such a vast array of people. I believe that the warmth and poignant memories contained within the walls of this house were the very reason why so many residents and others intimately connected with the house refused to move on from this place. From bandits to gamblers, high society folks and friends—their spirits lingered, captured by the undeniable pull of the house and all of the nostalgia contained within.

Though we could never truly anticipate the extent of our experiences with these spirits, we knew we were becoming an integral part of the home's mystery. After enough time passed, I came to realize and understand that we abided together in this special place, this Golden House on Silver Street.

CHAPTER 3

Celebrating Her Historical Splendor

> *"A lot of what this house contributed to our history, maybe vaguely known before, was now intensely felt and completely understood."*

We found great pride in the work we completed in our restoration of the house and grounds. As we renovated the property room by room, we were preparing for an art gallery to be situated in one wing of the house; it was an exciting and new experience for us. We would add more gallery space as we finished each room or area. By "finished," I mean brought back as close to the original condition as possible. The north wing was the first section of the main house to be done. It contained the living and dining area, a kitchenette, and a bedroom with an adjoining bath. There were front and back entrances accessible from the outside plus an entrance to the great room in the interior of the main house.

The outside areas of the property were no less spectacular in their prime. Each year, in early spring, the huge backyard became a fairyland. It was full of wild garlic bulbs. When they bloomed, the entire yard was blanketed with small periwinkle and white blossoms. It was just breathtaking. My husband had dug up the entire yard and, in the process of leveling it, the bulbs were distributed all over the property.

One day as he was clearing the back yard, he saw blue-green colored rock sticking through the ground here and there. We started uncovering some pieces and discovered they were slabs of ledge rock. We dug it all up and created pathways, patio areas, and framed in flowerbeds with it. I never saw anything this man set his mind to that he couldn't do—and do well.

He and John were going to hack out an old tree stump out back. He was drawing back the axe when John yelled, "Hold on, this doesn't feel right!" On closer inspection, it turned out to be a log of petrified wood. It was about three feet long and better than two feet wide. Someone, long ago, had set it on end so that it appeared to be just an old tree stump.

There was also a huge rock out back, about three feet by three feet. It was made up of crystals upon crystals on top of crystals, like a giant piece of geode. Someone kept sneaking in and chopping crystals off of it. We had to hire a small electric crane to lift it up

CHAPTER 3: Celebrating Her Historical Splendor

and have it brought inside so that it could be preserved. We did the same with the petrified log. They're still there for visitors to see.

In the interior of the home, my husband put his wonderful talents to work in salvaging an original door that had rotted, and he toiled tirelessly in stripping away the more modern layers of the home. My son John worked evenings after school and weekends right alongside us. Between the three of us, we ripped out all the layers of linoleum, sanded the original, rich old wooden floorboards, and then put a marine finish on them. We put light coats of sealant on the wood so you could actually touch and feel the wood grain. As layers of wallpaper were removed, we revealed a wooden box on the wall with a wooden door on it. We learned that this was the place where notes and mail, pony express mail no less, were placed when this wall was the outside wall of the house before the wing was added in the mid-1800s or so. We discovered this information via drawings and photographs that were shown to us by the former owner's family as well as in old newspapers and sketches. It was akin to discovering lost history!

The large main room of the house, or great room, was added for display. This required removal of seven layers of wallpaper, plus the wood paneling which lay on top of it, as well as removing a drop ceiling. Cracks and nail holes in the old wood of the wall in the middle room, which faced the great room, required countless repairs. The great room's facelift additionally included restoration to the adobe walls and the Santa Fe style doorway and flooring.

Later came the interior repair of John's room, the second oldest room in the house.

We decided to leave the wood flooring in the bathroom alone. This would enable visitors of the art gallery to see a sort of "before and after" view of our renovation work. The tall windows, with their antique glass, flooded the rooms with light. What a great place to begin our Customs House Gallery of Fine Art. It was truly a labor of love.

★★★

The gallery filled with art very quickly. We accepted art on a consignment basis, and the artists brought their work in for our consideration. We agreed to display the work for a specified period with the intent of selling the piece at an agreed-upon price. When, or if, the object sold, we received a percentage of the sale price from the artist for our services. If it did not sell, the artist simply picked up his or her work, often bringing replacement pieces for the same type of agreement, hence repeating the procedure. Thus, when no art was sold, we received no funds but still provided our services. As is evident, the scale weighed heavily in the artists' favor. Our time and the numerous expenses involved continued regardless of any art being sold or not. By no measure could it have been considered a profit-making business. It was more of a non-profit enterprise or rather an expensive hobby. At no point did funds received from sales come close to covering expenses, but we loved what we were doing, and we

CHAPTER 3: Celebrating Her Historical Splendor

were becoming what we hoped was a valued part of our Deming community.

Between the property's historical background, which we were constantly researching and adding to the known list of facts and legends, and the beautiful works of the talented artists who chose to use the gallery's services, our lives had definitely changed. We had set out to start a new adventure, and an adventure we had found.

At one point, we had a core group of twenty-six artists from all over the nation. We eventually expanded our offerings to include gifts, porcelain dolls, a "bed and art" overnight accommodation, U.S. Customs information pamphlets, and local and statewide tourist information of every kind. In essence, we offered everything we could conceive of to promote the assets we, and the area, had to offer to the public.

★★★

To say that I, or we, did this alone would be ridiculous. To tell you all of the stories of the literally hundreds of people who gave of their time, talents, personal purchases and donations of every sort, would truly be a book of its own. The salvation of this national, federal and state historic site is a real and true American love story.

Many people from every walk of life, every occupation, and every social status began joining us. The house inspired them individually and collectively and in every conceivable way you can think of to offer whatever they could to this "Grand Ole' Dame."

A clear example of the community love for this grand piece of history occurred one spring day in 1993. I was lying on my stomach, on top of the roof of the long portico that covered the public sidewalk in front of the house. I was semi-hanging over the edge while trying to put caulking in a cracked piece of wood. The crown-type molding that ran around the edge of the roof just above the support pillars was cracked and needed to be filled to keep out the weather.

Suddenly, I heard a very deep voice call out, "Hey Lady!"

I raised my head up to see a big, tall man in his sixties or so standing at the edge of the street down in front of the house. His hands were on his hips with his feet planted slightly apart. He was looking at me quite sternly. I had a suspicion that he was going to say, "You're using the wrong kind of filler on that wood." I knew that, but it was what I had and that was better than nothing, for now anyway.

"Are you trying to keep this place up on your own?" he yelled up.

"Sort of," I yelled back. "Don't you think she's worth it?" I said.

He looked down, was quiet for a few minutes, then looked up and said, "I took some pretty good molding off my mom's place when we remodeled it a while back. It's up in Minnesota, in a barn. When we come back down here next year, I'll bring it to ya. It's in a good bit better shape than what's up there now. Would you like to have it?"

I looked back at him and said, "Sir, I appreciate your offer, but I really can't afford it right now." (Hell, if I couldn't afford real wood putty, how was I supposed to swing crown molding? Ha! I laughed to myself inside.)

"Lady, who said anything about buying it? How about it being our way of just helping this old place to be around a few more years? I'll drop it off to ya next year 'bout this time, OK?"

Happily, I replied, "Yes, sir! Me and this house do thank you much!"

It was incredibly thoughtful and just another indication of the community love that was felt for this grand piece of history. There were those who fought anything they could not control, which of course only served to inspire the rest of us to fight for her harder than ever.

Somehow, the home seemed to become everyone's "Grandma's house." I cannot tell you how many times I heard, "Oh, this is just like the one that was in my grandmother's house." They were referring to the cast iron claw foot bathtubs or wide window seats or ceramic doorknobs. Sometimes it was the bay window and the rocker with the patchwork seat pad placed so that you could stare into the yard and daydream. Or maybe it was the geraniums and African Violets on the windowsills or the wooden French doors. I had utilized many of the antiques from my family, which had been passed down to me through several generations, in decorating the rooms. Warm, fuzzy memories brought that special look to their eyes. I just loved it and shared those warm fuzzies with them.

When they read the articles and looked at the pictures of her past that I had posted here and there throughout the house, they seemed to get a good feeling for all she had stood through and endured. The building of our country took on a kind of emotional reality when standing here, in this house. A lot of what the house contributed to our history, maybe vaguely known before, was now intensely felt and completely understood. They took her into their hearts!

The house possessed a kind of grandeur that enchanted you.

Events unfolded in ways that still mystify me. The snowballing effect of people joining in to get the house declared a historic site was something of wonder. Large numbers of U.S. Customs officials became involved, from the local agent in charge to the district directors, to the Director of U.S. Customs himself. On the day of the federal dedication of the house, hundreds of people came from all over to celebrate.

Senator Pete Domenici, a New Mexico native, took the time to chat and have a cup of coffee in our breakfast nook just to learn more about the history of the house.

CHAPTER 3: Celebrating Her Historical Splendor

Other high-profile government attendees included Senator Jeff Bingaman and Congressmen Steven H. Schiff and Joe Skeen, both from the U.S. House of Representatives. Even the president sent a representative. There were high-ranking Customs officials from all over the country as well as other political and official representatives from every rank and influential group in the state. CNN was present and shot footage that was aired during the daily news brief. Masses of local people turned out to see the ceremony including friends and artists.

The U.S. Postal Service even created a miniature post office inside the house and stamped special post cards featuring a drawing of the house on them, commemorating the event with a special stamp. Books and old ledgers were flown in from the Customs archives in Washington, D.C. and placed on tables and stands for people to look at, along with other memorabilia.

I recall a couple from El Paso, Texas yelling out with great delight at having found their great grandparents' names on the entry ledgers of the 1800s. We stood together afterwards and marveled at how all of the people involved, and there were many, had been able to pull together and get this job done, and done very well!

The celebration declaring it a federal historic site took place on April 22, 1989. I received a letter from Thomas W. Merlan of the State Historic Preservation Office, stating that they had been notified by the keeper of the National Registry, Jerry L. Rogers, that it was entered in the National Register of Historic Places on Feb 20, 1990. It was now officially declared a national historic site.

The state of New Mexico had initially issued a temporary state historical site declaration, and soon after the federal acknowledgement, they made it a permanent one. As you can see, many people had relentlessly worked to ensure her continued existence and secure her place in our history. I told you she was ENCHANTING!

CHAPTER 4

Something Is Not Right

> *"The house echoed with sounds of people walking in the living room, but no one was in there."*

The restoration of the Golden House on Silver street is only part of the story, however. Along with the celebrated historical significance and treasured past came a startling history of quite another kind. I learned over the years that you could not have one without the other in the Golden House. Her residents—both past and present—were here to stay.

When we moved in and got situated in the summer of 1987, we all quickly settled into the business at hand. My son John was off to high school to tackle his senior year. My husband and I started with the first job of building a shop in the garage as well as repairing and restoring the two guesthouses so that they could be rented out. Then it was on to the main house.

We needed to get an income flow established utilizing our talents in cabinetry and stained glass. It was also important for us to adjust to rural life and the new people in our lives. Our desire was to constructively immerse our talents, our funds, and ourselves in this small town we now called home. I believe that God gives everyone different talents. We had to see how the ones He had given us would mesh with the talents of those already living in this town. How, or what, could we do to become a welcome asset in this community? Little did we know, nor could we have guessed in our wildest dreams, what fate had in store for us all.

During one of our many trips back to our home in Arizona, which we made for various reasons, we realized that we truly missed our little Schnauzer pup, Chimi, whom we had left behind in Mesa to serve as a watchdog and companion to our daughter, Christine. As a result of our longing, we decided to adopt two little male Schnauzer puppies to bring back to Deming. Little did any of us know that they were going to give us our first clues of the presence dwelling within the house.

One evening, we were sitting on the sofa in the large main room with one pup next to me and the other next to my husband. At one point, they both jumped down off the sofa and ran over to an empty corner of the room where they started barking and

CHAPTER 4: Something Is Not Right

growling nervously. With their heads down and their tails up, they frantically ran back and forth in a semi-circle pattern. We tried to get them to stop, but they weren't having that. I got up to look, thinking it must be a mouse or something, but there was nothing there. They both carried on like this, much to our amazement, for about ten minutes. Finally calming down, they returned to us on the couch. We all looked at each other and made jokes to ease our odd feelings brought on by what we had just seen. These jokes, aimed at breaking the tension after an unexplained occurrence, became quite popular within our family.

★★★

Wanting to immerse ourselves in the community, we decided to join the local art council and get involved. We soon became more and more active in this organization and eventually accepted various positions on committees and the like. We met several people who were, at one point or another, connected to the house we owned. One couple that we met was related to Mr. Seaman Fields, the U.S. Customs collector who had purchased the house back in the 1880s. Descendants of his family had owned it for the entire one hundred years between his purchase and ours. We invited them to visit the old homestead.

The couple came over one evening, bringing with them a minister's wife who had wanted to see the old place. We spent a pleasant time together and proceeded to tour the house so that they could see all of the restoration that had been done up until that point.

We drank some coffee, exchanged pleasantries, and then said good night. Allen and I walked back in and sat down, discussing how great it was having the great-grandson of Seaman Field here in the house so many years later, telling us tales of when he was a little boy and other family stories. It was a lovely evening.

We had barely sat down when all the doors in the house suddenly slammed shut so hard that they made us both jump. By this time, we had started making a joke out of talking back to the imaginary forces we seemed to encounter in everyday life. So we asked, out loud, "What's the matter, Seaman? Didn't we serve the right coffee tonight?" A quick, dismissive laugh was followed by too long of a silence between us. We were still unable to share our real feelings about the nature of these occurrences.

John came home from school, during the first week, and related stories of how the kids had asked if he really lived in "that haunted house" across from the museum. His stories only confirmed what we had already been sensing. Still not ready to give too much weight to the matter, we all adopted the practice of joking, halfheartedly at times, about the "ghosties" in the house.

Allen and I had begun working in one of the guesthouses in order to prepare it to be a rental property. By this time we had discovered it had been built in 1903 and was the first schoolteacher's house. Ironically, it had housed schoolteachers most of the time ever since. Later, when we rented the house, a schoolteacher would often show up in answer to our ad or rental sign. As we

CHAPTER 4: Something Is Not Right

progressed with the remodeling, we kept hearing what seemed to be two ladies talking. We couldn't make out what they were saying, but we could hear their muffled voices and light laughter. We would go outside and walk the perimeter of the small guesthouse looking for the source of the voices, but there was no one. We would come back into the house, and the voices would resume. The "ghosties" struck again.

The main house was not immune to the unusual incidents. While eating dinner in the main house, the kitchen light would frequently come on and go off at different intervals. We would often wake up to find that it had come on in the middle of the night. My husband decided that it was probably a short somewhere in the wiring, so he rewired the lights. Afterward, we kept experiencing the same phenomenon of the lights going on and off on their own, so he just removed the light. It was one less thing to wonder about. There was too much of that kind of event happening already.

Sounds, sounds, and more sounds!

The house echoed with sounds of people walking in the living room, but no one was in there. The sounds of doors shutting somewhere in the house; no one there either. One morning I was lying in bed, just waking up, and I felt the bed give so I turned to say, "Good morning, darling," to my husband. No one was there.

I got up and searched for Allen. He was in the kitchen making coffee. I asked, "Did you just get up from the bed and come in here?" He answered, "No, why?" *Oh hell*, I thought to myself. *I am really losing it!* When I told him what I thought I had just experienced, he said nothing but looked very unsettled.

By this time, we were all experiencing peripheral movement in the house. Human nature being as it is, of course we would always turn to see what had just moved. Nothing was ever found, yet out of the corner of your eye, you kept sensing movement. This type of thing really makes you question your sanity.

★★★

With my daughter, Christine, away from home a lot due to her work and class schedules, we decided that we should drive up and bring Chimi to live with us. So, off to Phoenix we went. We all enjoyed our brief, but welcome, break from the "happenings" in Deming. John visited his old friends, and they traded school stories. We, in turn, visited with our friends and enjoyed the company of Christine so very much. We sadly missed our son, Mark.

Upon our arrival back home, our little Chimi, met the male she had been waiting for all of her life. Our little one-year-old pup totally adored her, and she him. We soon had three more pups and a constant circus of antics to enjoy.

★★★

We continued our daily restoration of the property ripping up layer after layer of linoleum and removing layer after layer of wallpaper. We spent hours sanding floors down to the original surface or ripping up and replacing rotted floorboards. Repairing electrical and plumbing discrepancies proved to be quite a challenging endeavor. The difficulty we faced finding replacement parts, due to the age of the structure, met head to head with our determination to truly restore the house as close to original as possible in all phases and in every part of the property. At one point, storms rolled through and ripped up some of the oldest trees on the property leaving big holes in the lawn. Oh, well—the trees became firewood.

The family room, complete with a big old fireplace, became a swimming pool during the first good downpour. Up to the roof we went and found the leak. Then it was re-shingling, hot tar, and interior repairs. The Oriental jade green paint I selected, along with the new oak trim and brick fireplace, made that one of my favorite rooms. It was so warm and cozy on a cold winter's night. Beveled wood spokes, combined with stained glass panels, became a type of room divider on one wall. The glass would pick up the fire's glow and create an absolutely enchanting experience.

My husband removed some old cupboards in the hall area between John's room and the bathroom area. He began to unveil the beautiful wainscot wall behind them. This had been a porch at one time and then incorporated into another room. This was the method of growth through which the whole house had been built. Each room was added on during a different period in history.

The beginning structure was an adobe room with twenty-four-inch-thick walls. The roof was flat, and each end of the roof had a Spanish façade similar to the style used in construction of the Alamo in Texas. The façades were, and still are, part and parcel of the house. We discovered this when we climbed up on the roof area and made our way to the windows on the front of the house directly over the long Portico style porch that covers the public sidewalk. We pried open one of the windows and crawled in, each holding the window open for the other. They were quite heavy, and the long counter-weights, on ropes, had been removed and laid on the attic floor.

After we made it in, we stood up on the very old rafters. The view was startling to say the least. There, standing tall before us, were the Mexican adobe façades. Ceramic insulators and cloth-covered wire for the AC and DC electrical system in the house ran separately across the attic floor. We made our way along, very carefully I might add, to peer through various openings in order to see the many additions. Behind the rear façade was a long tin or copper roof. This was above the kitchen area. Toward the north lie two more additions with a section of adobe wall jutting up between them. To the south were more additions. Little sections of walls stuck up here and there.

It appeared as though a large roof was set over the top of the older flat-top-style roofs, much like an umbrella. It was initially a peak style; and then at some point, another peak style roof was added

CHAPTER 4: Something Is Not Right

to form a "T" effect. One other flat top roof to the south and yet another, a little lower, lay to the west. An old ventilation pipe, which appeared to have been connected to a wood or coal burning stove, was lying around in the space. In case you are wondering how we could see so much, so clearly in an attic, let me explain. So much sunlight was pouring through the roof that we almost needed sunglasses! That fact did not escape our attention—we knew we would have to do some roofing repair.

It was obvious, after our attic adventure, that each room had been added on, one by one. Many rooms started as porches first, were then enclosed, and new porches were added. This is how the house expanded on down through the years.

★★★

The room my husband was working on, between John's room and the bathroom, was in the center of the house. The floor dipped there and you could see, in the walls and floor structure, the point at which it had once been a porch. He had cleaned up the wood and was up quite high on a ladder preparing the area prior to installing new wood molding at the ceiling and wall junctions.

I was in the kitchen when he came bursting through the double French doors to exclaim that a bat had been buzzing around his head up on the ladder and that someone had swept by the ladder and almost knocked him off of it. I started to laugh at these absurd statements until I saw his ashen-colored face and realized he was serious.

We went back into the room that he was working on and looked for any signs of what he had said happened. There was no bat in there! We looked around the room and then returned to the kitchen. I got him a cigarette and sat down at the table until he got quiet and felt like going over what had happened.

When I pointed out that there were no windows or openings in that room for a bat to get in, he simply looked at me straight in the eye and asked, "OK, you tell me what the heck was buzzing and whirling around my head? What brushed by so close to me, on my way down, that it almost made me and the ladder tip over?" Needless to say, I had no answer. He refused to go back into that room for almost two weeks. I don't think he ever felt truly comfortable in the house again.

We continued to labor over the restoration of the home and celebrate each small victory of our progress. Despite the sometimes-overwhelming sense that we may have been in way over our heads, and the disconcerting persistence of unexplained occurrences, we soldiered on in our quest.

CHAPTER 5

A Storied Past

*"Here in this place. In this house, my house,
is my favorite place in all the world."*
—Seaman Field

Though we were bolstered by our progress in the home and enchanted by her potential grandeur, we still harbored questions regarding her previous residents. We knew from our experiences with the unexplained phenomena in the house that there may have been some foul play in her storied past. Fueled by our desire to uncover some of the mystery surrounding the house, we decided to check out the stories we had heard about a recent suicide in the house. We went down to the courthouse and started looking up old records, titles, and anything else we could think of to give us some clues as to the true history of the house.

Unfortunately, the stories of a suicide in the house were confirmed. A report stated that a former owner had died of self-inflicted gunshot wounds in 1981. It had taken place in our bedroom. *Our bedroom.* The thought sent shivers down my spine.

My mind suddenly flashed back to a day in late October or early November when I had finally got around to scrubbing off some coffee-looking stains high up on the wall and the ceiling of the bedroom. They were splattered only in one section of the room. I recalled having gotten the tall ladder out to clean these stains as the ceilings were very high. With my little bucket of cleaning agent in hand, I climbed up the ladder determined to get that wall clean. I scrubbed the stain away and got the spots off, but I noticed something of a thicker consistency here and there. I went to rinse my cloth and watched with bewilderment as the water turned red. The thought ran through my mind, *Was it blood, tissue? Impossible!* Having previously worked as a secretary in a hospital operating department, I was familiar with the look of what I was seeing. I decided that I HAD to be mistaken.

But now, with this new discovery, the questions filled my mind. *What size gun? Where did she do it? Small caliber while lying in the bed? No, that was not possible with the splatter pattern that high.* Later investigations by one of our renters and a local microbiologist resulted in a confirmed type O-positive for the stains—which returned every year without fail in the month of October.

CHAPTER 5: A Storied Past

The suicide was not the only violent event to have taken place in the home. Later, much later, two psychics would independently give us their accounts of the death of a six-year-old child killed by marauders in the early 1800s. They both claimed that this child's murder was the source of the reoccurring stains in the room. They told us a bone-chilling tale of a pioneer family's home invaded by a group of marauders of mixed Indian and Mexican blood. These bandits killed and robbed up and down the border with no quarter spared to any and all in their path. (The house was the border of the United States and Mexico at that time in history when the area was part of the massive Arizona Territory.)

The psychics recounted a ghastly scene of bodies, many men and women, lying butchered in the backyard and corral areas. They related a tale of unspeakable horror.

> In the house, in that bedroom, the little blonde girl about six-years-old was grabbed from the bed where she and her mother were napping in the middle of the day. Her mother's screams filled the room as she was assaulted and then murdered. The child's screams and cries echoed along with those of her mother. By her feet she was swung. Her head met the wall over and over again until that little one, that dear innocent little one, ceased to cry, forever.

The story continued.

All was quiet now in the house. The bandits loaded up their new treasures and left. People came and saw what brutality had taken place. Word spread of the horrors that besieged this hard working pioneer family. Bodies, in the heat too long, were buried in that backyard in the spot where hedges now grew; all except one—the little girl. Her body rests in the curve of the sidewalk, in front of the bay window, with a statue of St. Francis holding a bird and flowers above her resting place.

It was unfathomable. But the story of the little girl did explain why my husband, not knowing what innocence lie beneath, had insisted that this spot was where a flower garden must go. I also knew, in the same sort or mysterious way, that the little statue of St. Francis, which my Mother had given me, belonged there, in the middle of the flowers. That is, if I could believe this tale which was told by one, and then another, who spoke of the same events.

We would soon find out that the hideous murder of that sweet little girl and her mother were not the only brutalities that took place in that room. French doors at one end of that bedroom, our bedroom, led outside to a former porch that was now enclosed and used as a workroom and storage area. In the bedroom, in front of these doors, the carpet would sometimes take on a red hue in a semi-circular area. At first, I attributed it to the sun coming through the red velvet drapes that hung in front of the doors leading into the workroom. But then the

CHAPTER 5: A Storied Past

red tone became noticeable later in the evening hours without the aid of the sun.

A local artist who stated that she had envisioned things in her mind's eye before said that she had seen a Spanish girl named Maria murdered in front of those doors. A Spanish/Indian man named Frank had slit her throat as she tried to flee from the brothel and gambling house that he was running there. She had been kidnapped in Old Mexico and brought there against her will, or so the story went. Her brother, who had set out in search of his sister, had finally found her. He told her to sneak out the French doors that led to the garden. There he would have horses for them to escape back to their home in Mexico. Frank had found out about their plan and, as she went to leave, he grabbed her by her long black hair and murdered her on the spot. Her brother was shot and killed at the same time by one of Frank's men.

Many of the occurrences I relate here are ones that were told to me. I want you, the reader, to know the difference between the things that I have personally experienced and ones that were related to me by others. You must form your own judgments as to the merit they deserve in the overall picture. Despite my desire to believe otherwise, confirmations of the stories of violence continued to appear.

One of those confirmations came from a lady who had hired us to do some cabinetwork in her home. One afternoon she came by to tour our house because of its historical significance. In the process of showing her the various rooms and relating some of the history of the house that we had discovered so far, we ended up in the master bedroom.

She asked if it was always so cool in this room. She was chilled. Before I could say much about it, she took my hand and said, "Pray with me." She began speaking words not understandable to me and then looked in my eyes and yelled, "Blood calls to blood in this room!" She turned around and left the house very quickly without another word.

She never returned, and we never spoke of that incident while completing the cabinetry job at her home. I did not mention it, as I did not want to upset her. She had health problems, and I often wished I had never offered the tour of the house, considering how the tour abruptly ended with that negative experience.

Many people, including my son Mark and his friends, have seen a man in a black hat in or around the house. With piercing eyes, his appearances were always late at night after the sun had gone down. The manifestations remained confined mostly to one of the bedrooms, the hallway (or the area between the rooms), or outside the house. Several people have spoken of him. This is the way that each has described him to me. Each time someone related a sighting to me, I remained quiet so as to get an untainted picture of their experience of him. Afterward, I would let them know that others had seen him also, and this helped them become less frightened. Although, I must admit, they usually moved away soon thereafter or stopped dropping by to visit.

★★★

Despite the horrific nature of some of the home's history, not all of the discoveries we made about the house were shrouded in such violence and terror. In researching the place's history via old records in the local courthouse, as well as in Silver City, we discovered so very much—not only about the house, but also about the whole geographical area. Information resources included many local residents, old newspapers, pictures (which were brought by the Field family for us to view and sometimes copy), the U.S. Customs people, more photos from a local historian (who was also an author and mechanic), and the various groups of people that came each year for what was called "Old Timer's Week."

Deeds to the property would show it changing ownership sometimes monthly and at one point even weekly. Tracking the chain of ownership was a hard one to figure out until the names started popping up in old news articles. It turned out that the town was a true Wild West gathering place. Lots of shootings, gambling, and every sort of activity associated with that time period in our country's history were witnessed on the property. To make a very long story a little shorter, the property was won and lost many times in the deal of a card! Of course, that's just my personal opinion, but I have formed it based on the multitude of what I have seen and read.

Some of the articles I spoke of referred to a lady gambler by the name of Lottie Deano. She was the daughter of a Mississippi and Ohio riverboat gambler. She was quite well known in gambling circles. It seems she met up with another well-known gambling figure of that time who went by the name of "The Cherokee Kid." His real name was reported as Frank Thurman. One article related how he and Lottie had a gambling house and Doc Holiday, the famous gambler (or infamous, depending on your point of view), visited their establishment on one occasion. Supposedly, the Cherokee Kid had lost all that they had to Doc when Lottie came out and proceeded to win it all back, plus a good bit more.

The Thurmans are also on the list of previous owners of this Golden House on Silver Street. Their graves are located in the town cemetery. The articles also stated that in their later years, they became great assets to their community performing many works of service and charitable deeds. They were respected members of the community and well loved by all.

I read yet another article that recounted an event in the mid 1800's when a local gambling parlor and brothel owner took a wagon full of his girls and dealers up to a nearby mining camp. One of the miners took advantage of his wares and then returned to his tent. Unfortunately for him, his wife smelled perfume on his clothing. When the man disrobed, she grabbed his pants and threw them into the campfire. Seemed like a good idea to her at the time;

CHAPTER 5: A Storied Past

however, she didn't realize that there were bullets in his pockets. Needless to say, after a few minutes in the fire, the bullets started exploding. The resulting report of the overheated cartridges sounded exactly like the camp signal used to alert miners of an impending Apache raid! This unintentional alarm resulted in mass pandemonium and a wild wagon race for the safety of the town. This story had been thus told in the local tabloid, with obvious amusement, referring to it as the "Great Apache Raid."

The multitude of articles that describe the shootings, hangings, and wild and wooly life lived there, and the forming of law and order and a new nation, would fill volumes. Some tragically sad, some wildly funny, and all truly fascinating testimonies to the interior strength, humor, and guts of those pioneer people.

I hung articles such as these on the walls throughout the art gallery along with pictures of the Field family and the house at various stages of growth and time periods. This included some classic time shots such as the "Dough Boys" marching by the front of the house. The building directly across the street had been an armory in the old days. It has a wooden running track, for the troops, suspended up on the third floor. I found this to be utterly amazing, architecturally speaking. It now houses a truly grand museum. This was also a wonderful source of information and pictures and articles. John Trowbridge, a great-grandson of Seaman Field (or "The Judge" as he was frequently called), and his wife donated many pictures and bits of family memorabilia to the research of this "Grande 'Ole House." The Trowbridges were a constant source of kindness and friendship.

The first records of the home depicted that it started off as a ranch, then a gambling spot, and then a border station for the Mexican government. Our government took it over in 1848. That is when it became a U.S. border station. Up until then, our border had been up the road about six or eight miles north. The records in Washington showed that the United States first began conducting Customs service in that location during that year. It was a Spanish town, at that time, named Rio Mimbres. Later, in 1881, it officially became Deming, New Mexico.

Captain Leonidas P. Steele was a delegate from Rio Mimbres in Grant County in the year 1868 (Luna County was formerly part of Grant County). An article from the San Angelo, TX Standard tells of an encounter with Apache Indians in the area. It seems they were having an election on February 28 of that year, and the Apaches swooped down and took seventeen of his horses and mules. He speaks of a wild chase, but the Apaches got away. The old railroad maps also show this area as Rio Mimbres Station on their line in 1880. The 1885 maps show the name changed to Deming Station.

Records show Seaman Field purchasing it from his son Robert in 1888. Robert's name had been on the deed since 1885. Members of his family owned it right up to the time that it was sold to us in 1987.

CHAPTER 5: A Storied Past

The U.S. government actually gave the whole town to the Wyandotte Indians in the north, by treaty, on March 17, 1842 and confirmed the ownership on January 31, 1855. It was recorded as "Float No. 9" in the treaty. Conflicting documents seem to tell a story of dual ownership by right possession and by legal title elsewhere. A man named Irwin P. Long conveyed it to a man named Albert A. Robinson in March of 1881. A man by the name of McCoy plotted the town of Deming out into streets, avenues, and blocks around 1881 and "civilization" began to take root.

SEAMAN FIELD

The Field family owned the property for the majority of its history. They had a storied past as owners of this treasured historical residence. The Field family had owned the property since 1885, over a hundred years before we purchased it.

Seaman Field was a man of many accomplishments. He was the Deputy Collector of Customs, by appointment of President Cleveland. This was the only office of its kind in the territory in 1894, and he held that office without bond, which was probably a first. Seaman was a member of the 33rd Texas Calvary. He began that career as a private and ended up a lieutenant colonel—a testament in itself to his skills and resilience.

He was a rancher and was engaged in real estate, mining, cattle, and insurance. Seaman was the first mayor of Deming and one of the first trustees. He also served as probate judge of Luna County. Continuing his military service, he was brigadier general commanding the New Mexico Brigade, Pacific Division, U.C.V. & S. and was one of the founders of the Adelphia Club. As if that weren't enough, he was president of the board of regents of the agricultural college (New Mexico State University) located in Las Cruces and was also a trustee on the local school board for six years. All of this and more was accomplished by a man described as having a meager formal education.

Seaman was born in New York. As a boy, he worked for his uncle as a clerk in his mercantile. He moved to New Orleans in 1849, where he worked as a traveling sales representative for a mercantile for about ten years traveling all over the south. He got married to Maggie and in 1862, enlisted in the Confederate Calvary, and transferred to Texas. When the war ended, he went back to New York and working for the mercantile. In 1876 he moved back to Texas. Sadly, Seaman lost Maggie, his precious Irish lass, in 1878. He later met Achsa and married her in 1881.

It was a good thing that fate brought them together. He would have undoubtedly needed help caring for the five children he and Maggie had together. At the time of his marriage to Achsa, Robert was eighteen, James was sixteen, Kate was thirteen, Jesse was ten, and Nellie was three years old. She surely had her work cut out for her. It must have been a hard adjustment for all.

CHAPTER 5: A Storied Past

Achsa was a fine woman and Seaman was a fine man; together they made it work. Albert was born in June of 1882 in Texas. Seaman, Achsa, and their six children moved to Deming, New Mexico later that year. This was the beginning of a new life and the formation of a legacy of pride and family that continues today. John and Barbara Trowbridge gave me a candy dish that had belonged to Kate. I treasure it highly. I feel honored to have it. Somehow, I feel it joins us together.

Seaman Field died on September 1, 1907. Achsa, his wife, died on January 26, 1927. Seaman and Achsa's son Albert lived with Achsa until her death. Albert and his wife, Mayelina, then became owners of the house. They had a son, Albert Killman.

Albert Sr. died on September 20, 1938. Mayelina lived on the property until she was elderly—at least that was what I was told by her family members. Albert Killman married a lady named Nancy Cross on July 5, 1932. They had a son named (you guessed it!) Albert Killman Field, Jr. This was a real challenge and source of confusion when I was researching deeds, legal papers, and such. Imagine ... three Albert Fields!

Albert Killman and Nancy were divorced in August of 1937. She remarried and so did he: she to a man by the last name of Rose and he to a lady by the name of Lauran Yates. Albert Killman, (or "Bony" which was his nickname), and Lauran had what was described to me as a real true romance, a special and loving marriage.

World War II was going on, and "Bony" joined many others in serving his country. The Bataan Death Marches took many men from Deming. This small town lost more men percentage wise than any other community in our country during that dreadful conflict. "Bony" was among those lost. Deming has a little park, across the street from the Golden House, with a marble memorial to these men who gave their last full measure for us all.

I thought of Lauran often, wondering how her feelings must have been in those years that followed. She did remarry and had a daughter whom she named Linda. That marriage didn't last, but she did have her daughter—someone of her very own to love. I am told that she had several problems in her later years.

God makes some to remain strong and some to run out of strength earlier than others. I often felt this might have happened to her. I am convinced she felt fearful in those last years of her life. Many of the windows, specifically the glass panes, in the house were painted with white paint. Perhaps the outside world frightened her, or maybe the "ghosties" played cruel games with her.

I have no way of knowing. I just always felt a closeness to her for some reason, as though she too endured loneliness in her days in the house by herself. I felt her with me sometimes. I had the same feelings about Mayelina, or "May" as most referred to her. I often thought of Achsa as well. We all seemed to have shared a common experience and goal: to keep the Golden House living, to the best of our individual abilities, each in our own time.

CHAPTER 5: A Storied Past

The house passed from Lauran to her daughter, Linda, and her husband, William (Bill) Schenk, Jr. Linda and Bill obviously loved the old place too. I found many places with signs of their touch to be seen. There were areas of cement where the name or initials of William Schenk were scribed in the concrete. Maybe they came and did these things to help Lauran or maybe they did them after she was gone? Either way, I believe that they struggled to keep the house going, just like all who have owned her did.

In my research on this glorious house, I came across so many mortgages by a great deal of her owners. It was real confirmation that they all struggled every bit the same, and sometimes more, than I did. This proved to me that she was enchanting to us all.

In some of the papers John and Barbara Trowbridge gave me, there was kind of a personal statement filled out by each of the various family members. With these documents, they were leaving a part of themselves for future generations of the family to read and thereby get to know their ancestors in a more personal way. What a truly wonderful idea. On Seaman's sheet, the question was, "If you could be anywhere in the world right now, where would it be?" His answer was not Paris or London. He answered, "Here in this place. In this house, my house, is my favorite place in all the world."

CHAPTER 6

Is This Really Happening?

"The footsteps, the doors creaked open and slammed shut, and things constantly moved from where you put them."

Throughout the period of several years, I experienced a roller coaster of excitement over our accomplishments and self-doubt regarding the paranormal activity in the home, despite the authenticity of what we were experiencing. I wondered about the stability of my faculties, and questions constantly ran through my head challenging my clarity of thought. You know, the things that make you say to yourself, *Hey dummy, get your brain in gear. Where's your head at? Boy, I must be losing it.* I sure wish that something as simple as, "getting my brain in gear," would have explained the happenings within the house.

I always had the feeling that someone else was in the house with me. Things were constantly being moved. I'd go to the store and return to find my carton of cigarettes, which I kept on top of the refrigerator, thrown all over the floor. Things were often found misplaced or missing. I kept securing the house more and more trying to prevent whomever I was *sure* was breaking in from gaining access. Even with all of the mounting evidence, I just didn't want to admit to myself what I already suspected and knew in my heart.

One day I was peeling potatoes in the kitchen. Suddenly, the bedroom door slammed, then I heard the sound of footsteps. I looked, but no one was there. Daily happenings such as these were frequent. One the morning I awoke to the sound of someone trying to get in my bedroom door. I was sleeping in the north wing of the house since it was more secure with locks, and I also slept with my gun for added protection. I could see two shadows at the base of the door; I guessed that they must be feet. I called out, "Please leave. I will shoot you if you don't, and I don't want to do that, so leave right now!" The knob stopped turning and I heard footsteps going away from the door. This was most certainly someone physically in the house, not ghosts or spirits.

The things I experienced on a daily basis were the types of little things that you first dismiss as memory loss or the result of stress or fatigue. But then they began to occur more often. They just could not be explained away as simple distraction.

CHAPTER 6: Is This Really Happening?

"Why did I put my hair brush in the cabinet? I never keep it there."

Then they progressed.

Where the heck are those cans of peaches I bought for our dessert today? I know I put them here in the pantry when I unloaded the groceries! Where else could I have put them? I remember setting them on this shelf, darn it! I know I put them right here. Well, they're not here now, are they? No, so start looking in the kitchen cabinets. Not there either! Could they have fallen out of the bags in the car? No, not there. Oh well, I must have left them on the counter at the store. Why are you getting so upset over a couple of cans of peaches? It's not the peaches; it's what's happening to my memory. Too many hours at this downright hard work. Arms ache, backaches, and I'm tired. Stop being so hard on yourself, ease up. Forget the darn peaches, stupid. Just get dinner on and then go soak in that great big old bathtub with lots of perfumed bubbles and call it a day. Yes!

I could not for the life of me find those peaches. I gave up.

Two days later, I went into the pantry to get the broom, and guess what? Two cans of peaches right where I had remembered putting them when unloading the groceries. Yeah, right! I began to imagine that there was some sort of trap door or other entrance into the house. Yep, someone with a sick sense of humor is coming in at night and when we are gone. That would explain the footsteps, the doors creaking open and slamming shut, and things moving from where you put them. That was the only reasonable answer. We all agreed that this must be the answer, and we all made a concerted effort to find this "secret entrance" into our home. No success yet.

It was very wearisome, to say the least.

I would sometimes awaken during the night to the feeling that someone had just sat down on the foot of my bed. I had the impression that one of them was guarding me as I also seemed to hear, in my mind's eye, the words, "Go lock the back door," or "Close the window in the kitchen." Each time, sure enough, I had indeed forgotten to do just that.

Because we had turned the left wing of the house into an art gallery, we had numerous art pieces hanging on the walls of the house. There were many, many times when we would leave the house on an errand, only to find every picture on the wall hanging very crooked when we returned. This could not be blamed on the windows falling and allowing the wind to blow through the rooms. They were Cape Cod style windows, so you had to manually open and close them. It was just another example of an occurrence that we could not quite wrap our minds around.

CHAPTER 7

Don't Mess With My Family

*"I'm here and I'm staying! This is my house now.
You're not going to run me off
or scare me off so get used to me."*

Back in the latter part of 1989 when my son Mark first came to the house, the events in the house began to intensify. When my older son John had lived there, he had many unnerving experiences. My husband, Allen, had experienced his share of unsettling occurrences, but he had now moved on to a new life since our divorce in early 1989. I had been alone in the house for several months. When Mark came back to Deming, the events became much more extreme, and he was constantly being harassed. The ghosties seemed to delight in making him miserable. The man in the black hat was constantly popping up and scaring him. It seemed downright cruel for my son, as well as for any friends he'd bring to the house. This truly angered me. I would not put up with this.

A friend of mine came over for a coffee late one afternoon. Mark was in the kitchen doing his homework at the dining table. She and I went to a local coffee shop to chat, and she left her dog at the house with Mark. He knew the dog, so he didn't mind. When we returned, my friend just stepped in, called the dog, and left. I turned to Mark and instantly knew something was very wrong. He was visibly shaken.

It seems that shortly after we left, he'd played with the dog and then settled back to his homework. The dog was lying at his feet, under the table, when all of the sudden she jumped up and stood between Mark and something unseen by Mark but surely seen by the dog. She stood erect and bared her teeth while snarling, growling, and barking. Then she sat back down only to jump back up and do it again. This went on, over and over, for the whole time we were gone.

The phrase "What was that?" became a commonly heard one in our house. Either Mark or I, or one of his school buddies (who rarely returned more than once or twice to visit him), were constantly finding a use for this phrase.

I knew that Mark was miserable in the house. His teacher, a local artist who used the gallery to show her work, told me that she felt that Mark was very unhappy.

CHAPTER 7: Don't Mess With My Family

As Mark's school year was approaching the halfway point, he had an altercation while working at McDonald's after school. A group of gang members tried to steal the Ronald McDonald House collection box, a donation box for sick children and their families. When they attempted to make off with the money, Mark literally leaped over the counter and took them all on. My young hero then became an object of gang retaliation. This was the tipping point. I made the decision to get him out of Deming.

I guess that in my heart, I knew this was coming. Very few were able to endure the constant events occurring in the house for very long. I was able to endure through the grace of God. By that I mean that I sought His help and protection constantly. Without it, I never would have been able to maintain the courage, or whatever you call it, to let the happenings roll off my back and in essence, say to the house's other inhabitants, "I'm here and I'm staying! This is my house now. You're not going to run me off or scare me off so get used to me. I'm the one who keeps this place from deteriorating and maybe becoming a public parking lot. So all of you had better work with me, got it?" Big words from this one-hundred-and-three pound female who found it necessary to leave on a regular basis to regain her physical and spiritual strength to continue. My Father's words stuck with me always: "Nothing is impossible if you want it badly enough."

★★★

We began to make plans to leave Deming after the halfway point in Mark's school year. However, the harassment of Mark and the general buildup of events were becoming much more intense. He slept on the daybed in my room a lot now.

We learned that the granddaughter of Seaman Fields had passed away not long ago, and then the last remaining child of Nellie Bell Fields and Walter Guiney, Seaman Guiney (Seaman's namesake) passed away too.

Soon after the realization that I would have to move Mark away from Deming, I awoke about midnight to sounds of a party going on. I could hear people laughing, the sound of music playing, and glasses tinkling. Robust laughter and voices chattering away filled the air. I couldn't make out what they were saying, but it was obvious they were having a grand time! I laid there listening and after quite a long while, I heard Mark whisper, "Mom." There was a pause and then, "Mom, are you awake?"

"Yes son, I'm awake."

"What's all that noise?"

"Sounds like someone's having one heck of a party to me, son."

"When are they going to knock it off? I've got school tomorrow."

I looked at the clock again. It was two-thirty now! I thought, *Yeah, he's right. This has gone on long enough.* I decided to get up and go tell them to quiet down so we could get some sleep. Enough is

CHAPTER 7: Don't Mess With My Family

enough! I got up, grabbed my robe and my revolver, and went outside to find which neighbor was having the party.

My bedroom was located at the front of the house, so I went out the front door. I really thought the party was probably kitty-corner from the house, at the house on the corner by the park. Those people often had large gatherings.

When I got outside, not a sound! *What? It must be someone else,* I thought. So I proceeded to go around the house to the back. Nothing! I walked up the double drive, past my renters in the guesthouses. No sound anywhere! I went back around to the front. Still no sound. When I got back in the house, I could, again, hear the party going on. By this time, Mark was up and worried about me. I assured him that I was alright, but I couldn't find from which house the noise was coming. We decided it must be coming from the City Hall or the surrounding homes.

The size of the lot that our house sat on was almost a quarter of a city block. Maybe I just hadn't walked back far enough, I thought. I went out the back door this time and through the gate to the double drive. I proceeded back to the garage and then down the side to the back wall. Nothing! I stood there with my gun in my hand and peered into the back lot of the doctor's office and across the adjoining lots trying to see or hear something. Still nothing!

I made my way back into the house to face a young boy, whom I loved so dearly, and put my arm around his shoulder and jokingly told him, "Guess what, the party is in our house!" Of course, he had to go out and listen to the "quiet" too. I don't know what time it finally stopped. We both eventually fell asleep with it still going on.

The following day, the wife of the Fields' great grandson, who was renting one of the guesthouses from me, stopped me in the back to tell me she had seen me outside the night before with my gun in hand. She made the comment, "Guess they were celebrating all of them being together now." I realized that she was probably right. Seaman was the last of the grandchildren to die with his wife passing just a little while before him. I asked her if she had heard it too. She just looked at me intensely and silently shook her head up and down.

★★★

Another night, we were entertained by what seemed to be a bunch of wagons, horse drawn wagons no less, rolling by the front of the house. It was a similar scenario:

"What is that?"

"I can't tell, son. What does it sound like to you?"

We got up and looked out the window. Nothing there!

We lay back down and listened to sounds like horses' hooves complete with a little whinny now and then, chains (or rather harnesses) clanking, and a "thump, thump, thump, thump" sound.

CHAPTER 7: Don't Mess With My Family

Finally, a crack like a whip was heard, and we both yelled, "Wagon trains!" Watching old movies on TV was good for something other than passing time after all.

★★★

One weekend before Mark's first semester of school was finished, Mark went with me to Tucson to look for a place to stay. Saguaro High School was well known for its sports programs, and he felt that he might like it there. We finally found a place and went back home to get ready for the move. The time was definitely right to go; it would be a much-needed change of scenery for us both. We started packing up what we needed to take and began counting the days until school was out for the winter holidays and our Christmas present to ourselves (our move) could be enjoyed.

We very quickly perceived that the ghosties didn't like the idea. There developed a thickness in the atmosphere of the house. I could compare it to the feeling you might get in a large crowd. You have your own space, and yet the activity around creates a feeling of anticipation or caution. A definite increase in sounds and peripheral movement were noticed by us both … all the type of happenings that elicited a "what's that?" comment.

The night before moving day turned into a nightmare; it was truly one of my worst experiences in the house. Two young men were coming the next morning to help load up the moving van that I'd rented. We were both excited about the move and weary from getting ready for it. It was just before Christmas, and we would be in our new place for the holiday. It was a very cold night, so we had two of the sofas placed at right angles to each other in the bedroom by the gas furnace. Because there was no central heating, each room had its own little furnace. My sleeper was in front of the French doors and Mark's sleeper ran along the windows. Both sofas sat two or three feet from the walls. In this configuration, we both received the benefit of the heat. The door to the bathroom was a few feet from the foot of my bed, and the door to the main room a few feet from the foot of Mark's.

Sometime during the night, I awoke and sat up in sure knowledge that something was wrong. I felt the presence of evil behind me. This feeling was utterly overwhelming. I told myself, "Stop this. It's just your nerves. Stop it!" My hair literally stood up away from my scalp. The feeling built, and I could feel something wishing me great harm. Evil was behind me in front of those doors. I summoned up my internal strength, and it took all I had to turn around and look. Its breath was upon me! I made the sign of the cross and ordered it to leave. "In the name of Jesus Christ, Son of the Most High, I order you to leave here now!"

I speak to you, dear reader, to reaffirm that these were indeed my feelings. I cannot express how intense they were. There are simply no words to fully express them. They fully enveloped my entire being.

I turned my back on the evil entity and sensed the "regulars" of the house were gathered over by the door that went into the main

CHAPTER 7: Don't Mess With My Family

room. I felt they were cowering there, looking at me. I turned around again and said, loud and clear, "In the name of Jesus Christ, your boss's boss, I order you to depart this house and not return, ever!" I repeated this over and over. The nightmare feeling finally ceased. I turned back and looked at Mark. He had sat up and was looking at me. He closed his eyes and, without a word, he laid back down and began to sweat profusely. I laid back down and slept.

By morning, Mark was running a temperature of 103 degrees. I took him to the emergency room. It was obvious that he was very ill. Lab tests said that something had gone amok in his system, but they couldn't tell what it was yet. They were never truly able to say exactly what it was. The doctor said it could possibly be a kidney stone or maybe a virus. No real answer ever appeared in the tests. After three days, whatever it was finally left him. I could bring him home to our new place in Tucson.

★★★

Mark finished out his year at Saguaro High School, and we moved back to the Golden House after Mark's graduation. He only had a short time before he would be starting his enlistment in the U.S. Navy, so we bided our time in Deming. In just a few weeks following our return, the place started getting so eerie and the strange occurrences began to take over our everyday lives again. We were not doing well. He moved back to Mesa briefly, but that didn't work for him. He worried about me too much.

We had been up to visit my daughter Christine, and Mark asked if his friend could return with us to New Mexico for a visit. We picked up his friend and returned home. Art was the same age as Mark. I thought that this might make the waiting period before Mark left for military boot camp go a little faster for him.

Things did not go well. The man in the black hat seemed to constantly appear and frighten the boys. I moved into the north wing and gave the boys my bedroom. The man in black bending over them was a familiar complaint heard from them. One or the other (or sometimes both of them) would start yelling and running to me. It got to be a common habit for them to carry the mattress from their bedroom into the family room. They would watch TV and just fall asleep there. I often heard them call from the room, "Mom, he's at the back door again. His eyes are glowing!" I really figured that their imaginations had run amok and would joke them into laughter as much as possible.

One evening, we were all in the family room and the boys were watching television. I decided to go to my quarters early. I said good night and headed for my wing in the house. As I went through the kitchen, Mark was following me on his way to the sink for a drink of water. We were chatting on the way. I said the usual, "Don't stay up too late and don't forget to turn off the TV." I was in my room less than a minute or two when I heard Mark yelling, "Art, stop it! STOP IT!" I hurried back into the kitchen to find out what was going on now.

CHAPTER 7: Don't Mess With My Family

Mark had both hands pressed against the pantry door. He was pushing and yelling, "You're breaking the door! Stop it!" I could see the light in the pantry was on and the screws of the door were being pushed out of the frame side of the hinges. Someone was pushing so hard to get out of the pantry that the wood of the doorframe was starting to crack.

I yelled at Mark to let go. I asked what the heck was going on. He started telling me that he was just kidding with Art who was in the pantry and it had just gotten out of hand. As he was talking, Art appeared at the other end of the room coming through the French doors.

"What's going on?" he asked.

Mark turned to me, looked totally confused, then went white in the face and started to shake.

We stepped back, opened the pantry door, and found no one in there. In reviewing what had happened, Mark related how he followed me up to the front to the sink, got his drink, and as he approached the pantry area, the light was on and the door swung out at him. He assumed Art was in there and was trying to make him walk into the door or literally smack him with the door.

Mark decided to reverse the joke by pushing the door back, thus trapping Art in the pantry. Then whatever or whomever he thought was Art started pushing from the inside so hard that the hinges began coming off, and the door frame started to crack.

That is when I heard the yelling and came in. *What's wrong with this picture?*

We discovered that Art had actually gotten up and used the bathroom after Mark and I got up and went our respective ways. This leaves us all with the question of *who* turned on the light in the pantry. What force pushed that door so hard from inside the pantry to cause the very obvious damage? Who swung the door out towards Mark as he was approaching it on his way back to the family room?

After much talk, and even after the trauma of the pantry event, we decided to call it a night again. About ten minutes later, two very upset boys were banging on my door yelling. The man in black was back, peering at them through the screen door in the family room. They asked if they could stay in my wing of the house with me. "Ok," I said. Maybe we'll get some sleep some time tonight.

However, the events of the night were not over yet. The bouncing ball started. By bouncing ball, I'm referring to a little round spot of light about the size of a nickel that would periodically appear on the east wall of the bedroom in the north wing. At night, it would just appear and jump around on the wall, up near the top, then "whoosh" down to the bottom of the wall and then hop along or sometimes zigzag here and there. Sometimes it would jump to another wall. I often went to sleep having given up trying to find the source of this little moonbeam that got trapped in there. It freaked out the boys. They were just finally drifting off, after

CHAPTER 7: Don't Mess With My Family

accepting that new interruption, when thunder and lightning started crashing and resounding through the walls. *Will this night and the nonsense ever end?*

We finally made it to the morning. Thank God. I got up, as quietly as possible, and opened the door into the great room and got another jolt. Lying there, on the floor in the middle of the room, was the big picture that I had hanging over the bookcases—which, mind you, were more than five feet away. The glass was shattered. I cannot imagine how it got to the middle of the room. If it had fallen, it would be beneath the bookcase. The long, large nail that held it was still in the wall. The twine on the back of the picture was still intact. The frame was a very heavy, antique oak.

I was cleaning up the mess when the boys emerged, saw the picture, and freaked out again. Things like this, out of the ordinary and unexplained, continued until we finally decided to leave again. I took the boys back to Phoenix—Art back to his parents and Mark to stay with some friends. In 1991, Mark entered the U.S. Navy. I left Phoenix, went back to Tucson, and visited with a friend for a while before returning to New Mexico, once again.

CHAPTER 8

Experiences of Others

"It's alright, don't be scared."

Just as the fascination and love of the Golden House on Silver Street was not limited to our own family, the experiences surrounding the paranormal activity in the house were felt and related to me by many others at one time or another.

One of my many tenants while I owned the home was a border patrol agent who lived there alone for quite some time. He found the ghosties interesting and not frightening at all. He had more of an "I'll be darned" attitude toward the things that went on in the house. He told me that he had the feeling that the house was alive in the sense that he knew he wasn't alone when he was by himself. I could relate to that just fine. He said that he had felt someone sit down on his bed at various times.

His wife was originally from Texas, and they had married only a few months back. His experiences increased tenfold in the period after they married. His wife was not of the same nature as he was. She did not appreciate the unique happenings of the house. I really wonder if the ghosties didn't enjoy teasing her because of it. On one such occasion, while checking on her daughter in the bedroom, the wife came upon a man in a big black hat bending over her daughter as she slept. He looked up at her, and she noticed that his eyes were very bright and intense. She was very unsettled, to say the least.

Their experiences while in the house were quite varied. They said that one night they thought they heard their daughter saying, "I'm scared, I'm scared." The wife rose up in bed and saw a little girl coming into the bedroom through the bathroom door and realized it wasn't her daughter at all! It was a little girl in a long white gown with pink ribbons on it. She had long blonde hair and appeared very frightened. The husband sat up and saw her too. They said that when they realized it was a spirit, they told her, "It's alright, don't be scared." She stood by their bed for a moment, then went back into the black recesses of the bathroom and was gone. They both got up, turned on the light in the bathroom, and went into the adjoining room to check on their little girl. There they found her asleep in her bed wearing her white nightgown; however, no pink ribbons.

The wife also told of a little old lady whom she often saw fixing coffee at the sink in the kitchen. She said she would just be standing there, smile, and then be gone. One evening, after putting her

CHAPTER 8: Experiences of Others

daughter to bed, the wife entered the kitchen only to find several people with the old lady, all drinking coffee by the bay window. They all looked at her and smiled and then were gone. She mentioned that a man with a long red beard was there with the others. The man with the red beard is a spirit that I would consider another "regular," common to the stories related to me by many who have seen him. The wife's anxieties multiplied to the point where they truly had to do something, for all of their well-being.

In order to try and suppress the activity in the house for the sake of the family, I had a local priest, a gentle man in his fifties, over to bless the house twice. He left me some holy water and showed me how to use it when things got out of hand, so to speak. After blessing the house, he became plagued with anxiety and his health slowly deteriorated. He finally ended up leaving the priesthood. I always felt bad in the sense that I hoped it wasn't the house entities that had affected him so badly. I will never know, but I still pray for him.

The couple called me to come over and "de-ghost" the place a couple of times with the holy water, but the buggers wouldn't knock it off so the family decided to move. Shortly before they moved, the intensity of movement, sounds, and appearances increased, and the walls started to spot up again.

The husband took a sample with a knife and gave it to the microbiologist I spoke of earlier in this book. He said that it smelled like blood to him. The scientist tested the sample for both of their sakes and confirmed that it was, indeed, a sample of blood. She had experienced various occurrences in the house while she was a tenant, so they got together to do this testing. I was unaware of this until much later when she told me about it. It had confirmed what I had suspected while washing the wall that first time.

One night, near the end of their stay in the house, they told me of a "banshee" type figure who was screeching and moving fast around the bedroom finally landing on top of the husband, who was in the bed. The figure tried to put a sheet or something on his head. He felt that it was trying to smother him, so he fought it. This really shook them up so badly that they felt that they could no longer stay in the bedroom, or the house for that matter. They brought the mattress into the family room and slept there. They moved before the month was out.

When the border patrol agent and his family were finally moving out, some men came to help them move. One of the men said that he was standing by the sink in the kitchen when a cup flew out of the cupboard at his head. He was quite upset, understandably. The border patrol agent and his family were relieved to finally leave the house.

★★★

Another border patrol family, who lived there for a brief time, complained of excessively large heating bills. It seemed that the bills were excessive because they were cold, all the time. I never

CHAPTER 8: Experiences of Others

knew what all had happened while they were there, but I did see that their heating bills were very expensive. The next thing I knew, they were gone and a single man was moving in to take over renting the place.

Another couple had moved into one of the guesthouses. The lady came to my door one morning, smiling timidly, asking if I'd like to have coffee. She announced that they knew the place was haunted. She felt them all the time and said that they played little games with them at night. Neither she nor her husband seemed scared, but they also moved within a couple of months.

Many of the renters I had moved rather quickly. I heard things like, "We will be moving in two days. We have jobs somewhere else." I'd like to believe that was true. I'm sure that in some cases it was and others, I'm not so sure. All of my renters were nice people and left me with good memories, and I always felt that we parted as friends. They were good people, all of them.

★★★

An artist friend, who was ill and unable to work at the time, needed a place to stay. She asked if she could move in and look after the house while I was in Tucson with Mark finishing high school. She loved the place also. This seemed like a good idea for both of us. Not too long after, her son and family moved in with her.

One morning, I got a call from her. She asked if I had some visitors in Tucson. I didn't know what she meant. She chuckled and said,

"Has anything unusual been happening?" As soon as she asked, I thought of the morning before when I had gotten out of bed and felt something cold under my foot. Looking down, I discovered that I was standing on a dime. I went into the bathroom and felt it again, looked down, and there lay two dimes. I went into the kitchen to make some coffee and found more dimes on the floor by the sink.

A tour of the place turned up more dimes in the other bath. I got to laughing. This was the type of thing that my son would do. He loved teasing everyone. When he came home from school, I said, "Okay, what's the message with the dimes?" thinking he'd probably say something like, "Oh, you found some money? I guess that means we should go out for a coffee and some pie, don't you think?" Instead, he looked at me and said, "What are you talking about?" We just looked at each other and said, in unison, "They're Back!" and laughed.

So, in answer to her question, I related the dimes episode. Her response was, "Since you found seven dimes, that probably means that seven of them came to see you." She then told me that the night before, she woke up and a little old lady was standing by the window in the bedroom. The lady said that she was going up to see Rosie. That was her nickname for me.

During that same conversation, she also told me that she had awoken one night to the sound of piano music coming from the main room. She got up and when she looked in the room, she saw a wedding going on. She entered the room, and no one seemed to notice her, so she sat down on a chair, next to a little

CHAPTER 8: Experiences of Others

girl, where the people attending were seated. The little girl was fussing with her sandal, and her mother reached over and fixed it for her telling her to "hush." She saw a man with a red beard and a slender dark haired girl getting married. Another reddish haired lady was playing the piano. She told me the people's names that she heard but I didn't write them down. She also spoke of a gray-haired man with a dark gray or salt and pepper beard being there as well. She said that she had seen him before when she had visited the house. He was always near me when she saw him. She had the impression that he was guarding me. I could relate to that as I often felt someone's presence in the house. Speaking with my artist friend and hearing her stories was just more confirmation that what I had been experiencing in the house was not in my mind.

Another friend of mine had several experiences in the latter years of my owning the house. She would stop in and check the place out every day or so when I was living away from Deming. She related to me that the Cape Cod style curtains in the kitchen were constantly being opened after she had shut them. Things were occasionally being moved or thrown around also.

Now, she has a bit of a temper which surfaces when she feels that someone is trying to play games on her. Whatever, or whoever, it was that kept doing stuff like that was really getting her dander up. She is a person of very unique and admirable qualities, one of which is a totally fearless attitude toward life. She meets, and enjoys, all of life's challenges. She seems to welcome each day with such a zest that it encourages all who are privileged to have her for a friend. One always feels secure with her in the sense that she leaves no doubt as to how she views any person or situation. When, or if, that person or situation changes in a significant way, she has no problem changing her opinion or attitude about them. This, I personally feel, is a rare and wonderful virtue in anyone.

It was because of these great human qualities that I found it no surprise to find a handwritten note addressed to "whatever son of a bitch who's messin' with the curtains and such in this house." The note continued, "This is to inform you that I'm armed and dangerous and will blow your bloody head off if I catch you in here. Since I come often, as you must know, watch it, Buster, because I'm bound to get ya before too long!"

She expressed a real frustration to me, on more than one occasion, concerning the occurrences experienced in the house. One thing for sure though, she never allowed fear to rule her actions. This was a fact that always impressed me and encouraged me to meet these events with a sure and strong faith in my own abilities to remain steadfast. She often came and stayed with the boys (whichever one was with me at the time), whenever something required me to be somewhere else overnight. Both of the boys and I were grateful for the company. We shared some fun and certainly interesting times up until she moved away. I missed her a lot.

CHAPTER 8: Experiences of Others

On one occasion, my daughter's boyfriend, Paul, came down with her to visit. We were in the kitchen talking, the three of us. There is a little breakfast bar where Christine and I were talking. Paul was at the sink getting a drink of water when all of a sudden he doubled over. I knew something had happened but I didn't know what had happened. He excused himself and said that he had to go to the bathroom so we assumed that he must have had a cramp or something. After some time had passed, Christine went to see if he was alright. They were gone quite a while. Finally, I got up and went to see what was going on at which that time they both came walking out visibly upset. Paul related that someone had kicked him between the legs. I looked at him and said, "What do you mean? You had a cramp or something?" He said, "No. I felt kicked. I felt somebody hit me hard between the legs and that's what doubled me up." Paul has had a great deal of difficulty staying in the house or coming to visit since that point in time. He is firmly convinced that he was hit or kicked between his legs.

★★★

A lady friend of mine used to come over once in a while to have coffee with me. She said that every time I left the room to answer the door bell in front or just left her presence for any reason, the canisters and various things sitting on the counter by her would start jumping around on the countertop. She swore that this happened every time I left her. She also said that the pantry door would start swinging open and shut until I returned.

One day her son came by to pick something up for her. We were standing in the main room talking when a friend of mine's dog, which was in the kitchen, started to howl mournfully. Her owner had left her with me while she ran an errand. I suppose she was just howling because I left her alone. He turned pale and inquired, "What was that?" I assured him it was just a dog in my kitchen. I couldn't help but start to laugh. It did sound very strange. He refused to believe me and said, "How do you stand these things going on all of the time? My mom says she sees things happen every time she comes over here." I had to take him back to the kitchen and show him the dog. We've laughed about that more than once, my friend and I. It was one on the few times I ever saw her son serious. He loved to tease everyone. I guess that's what made it so amusing.

One of my son John's friends, who later became a friend of Mark's too, told me he was always sensing movement around him. He also told of a time when he turned to see what was moving and saw a spiral of smoke in the area by the bathroom door. He said it just hung there and then moved off into the dark of John's room. He also felt very uncomfortable in the house. He was, and is, a dear and treasured friend to us all. He wouldn't come in very often but would drop by or call to see if I needed anything. I often referred to him as my number three son.

★★★

A very dear and gentle man of Mexican descent came by one day and told me that he had done a lot of work on the house for the

CHAPTER 8: Experiences of Others

daughter-in-law of Seaman Fields, way back in the 1930s. He had heard me mention a serious problem that I had regarding a wooden beam within the structure, and he told me that he had stopped by to take a look at it for me. We became good friends over time. Though he was in his mid-eighties, we found much to talk and laugh about. His carpentry skills were well known, and he seemed to thoroughly enjoy doing things around the place. Each room had a story to it regarding the Fields family. He shared stories of what they had him do in the room or of something that was said. Sometimes he would come over in the evening, and I'd make popcorn and we would talk and talk. It was nice to share my time with someone who understood and appreciated both the historical nature of the home and its many eccentricities.

He related to me, once, how the movement he had noticed in my house had somehow transferred over to his house. He told me that a man, whom he had often hired, came over to do some yard work. He found the man nervous and frightened when he had returned to see how he was coming along with the chores. The man was packed up and ready to leave even though he wasn't done with his work. My friend asked why he was leaving, and the man said that he had heard noise coming from inside of the house. He had gone over to the window and looked in only to see the furniture moving all about the room. He was so upset that he never came back. We joked about it, but it was a real concern to him. I saw it in his eyes.

He was a real special person to me, and his kindness and help in surviving those trying years will never be forgotten by this lady. He was there when I found myself unable to do the things that needed to be done by a stronger, more construction-minded person. I was there for him with a listening ear and an understanding heart that heard and felt his loneliness. How much better can a friendship get? We both felt that we came away better for having known each other.

★★★

A couple that I had been friends with for several years, Gracie and Don, would come down and visit me every now and then. They lived in Arizona. On their first trip down to see me, she came to tell me of a strange experience she had in the backyard. She was sitting on a lawn settee looking at the flowers and the St. Francis statue when a little blonde-haired girl, about five or six, came around the corner of the house and walked up to her side. She said the child looked so sad. She was wondering who she was and at the same time automatically reached out to comfort the girl when her head began to throb and pain something fierce. Her face and head were throbbing and stinging but only on the right side. Then the child was just gone and she didn't see her go. She thought the child had pushed against her head so hard it had hurt her. However, there was no mark on her face or head to explain the pain that she was feeling.

Don later made mention of seeing a man in a black hat and two other men, both with long beards. One had a reddish beard and hair and the other; a salt and pepper colored beard. He said that he had seen them just wandering around the backyard in the late evening hours.

Don and Gracie returned at a much later date with a woman from Canada named Dorothy. While meeting and getting to know her, the couple had relayed their experiences at the house to her. They decided that they would come back down and show the woman the house. From things they told me later, they had some very intense happenings in the backyard one night.

On that particular night, they felt a great deal of movement and unsettling feelings outside, like being surrounded by a multitude of people. The three of them formed a circle in the yard around an intense light through which the spirits could go to leave this world.

They encouraged the spirits to move on through the light, but they had a hard time with a little girl; Gracie said this was the same little girl who had made her head hurt while she was sitting on the bench the one day. Ironically, I knew her as the little girl who the psychic had told me was murdered by having her head smashed against the wall. They all kept calling to her to go through to the light, and she finally ran through.

A little Spanish girl by the name of Maria was also very nervous and frightened to move on. They had to cajole and encourage her to move through the light. She, too, finally ran through the light. In fact, she raced through so fast that it hurt Gracie's chest.

I just want to mention here that I don't know anything about these things. I'm just repeating what I was told. Maybe someone who is into these kinds of phenomenon would better understand the feeling Gracie encountered when the spirit ran through her into the light.

Don told me that the man in the black hat, black beard, and dark piercing eyes was also there that night in the backyard. He was a real nasty one. (I assume this was the same man in the black hat that had been seen by many others and had terrorized my sons and their friends.) They got the sense that he did not want to go. He kept circling them for over an hour before he went through Dorothy into the light.

Many others passed through into the light that evening, but some did not. After that experience, all three felt very peaceful, in direct contrast to the commotion and unsettling feelings they had experienced earlier.

Dorothy went back home with some strange tales to tell. They felt that their experiences were both exciting and more than a little unnerving. They really believe that some of the ghosties passed through their bodies into the light during their time in the backyard.

I have not had these kinds of experiences personally. I cannot explain them, but only recount them to others as they were told to me. I cannot swear to the validity of the matters that I have related to you except for the things that I have experienced myself. The things that I have, and will tell you, the reader, were told to me and are yours to interpret as you choose.

CHAPTER 9

Paranormal Events Intensify

*I clearly heard the words,
"Leave here. Leave here NOW!"*

On September 17, 1991, I began keeping an audio journal recording my experiences in the New Mexico house. I used my old-fashioned cassette tape recorder to accomplish this task. I had just returned to Tucson where I had rented a small apartment. I was hoping to find work to help with all of the expenses of the Deming House. I decided it was time to start keeping a journal or some type of record of all of the strange events that had been, and were still, going on in connection with the house.

Prior to this, I had been at the house for four days. A refrigerator in one of the guesthouses had gone bad, and I also had some plumbing problems to address. Luckily, I had been able to get the refrigerator repaired and running again, to my tenants' great relief. The plumber was due to return on the seventeenth, and I had about two or three more days' worth of work to do to finish up the present upkeep needs. I had trimmed all of the hedges around the main house and the guesthouse. The lawn could wait for tomorrow! In addition, I had repaired the missing shingles on the roof and put a new coat of waterproof sealant on the little roof over the laundry room.

It was about six or six-thirty in the evening when I decided to call it a day and put the hedge trimmers back in the garage. I was hot and sweaty with blisters on my hands. I retired to my little apartment, which encompassed the entire north wing of the main house and had its own entrance and exit doors, a patio, and a private living space. It also contained a living room, a bathroom, a bedroom, and a 1930s style compact kitchenette. The unique feature of the kitchenette was that it was a self-contained, stainless steel unit with a sink, cupboards, stove, and small refrigerator all together in a closet type arrangement with doors that closed to hide all of the amenities. It simply looked like a cupboard in the wall.

I grabbed a cold pop and went around the corner into the living room to my rocker, plopped down, and lit up. I sat there contemplating how good those fresh tomatoes, which I had bought earlier that day, would taste for dinner. I was looking forward to a hot bath, some television, and that good old bed. Thank you,

CHAPTER 9: Paranormal Events Intensify

God. Work had gone well and I was tired, but a *good* tired. How I loved that beautiful place!

As I sat and enjoyed the much needed rest, I looked up at the wall opposite of where I was seated and saw a kind of cross on the wall. The cross was the shadow of the wooden frame that formed the screen panels in the back door reflecting on the wall. The sun was just starting to set and was shining full blast on the wall across from me. I continued rocking in the chair and enjoying my time of mellowing out after a hard day's work.

Time for another smoke, I thought. I glanced down to get my smokes and when I looked up, there was a policeman at my back door. I couldn't see the door from where I was sitting, but his reflection was clearly seen on that same wall with the shadow of the cross.

I could see his hat with the characteristic bill as he was standing in profile with the sun bouncing off of his sunglasses. I got up to see what he wanted and when I reached the corner of the room, he was no longer there. In fact, there was no one there!

I went back and sat down. But the image that I had been seeing was still there. *He was still standing there*. His hand came up and removed his glasses. I rose up and peeked around the corner of the wall; no one there. I sat back down. The image remained. He then turned face forward, and his face seemed to change into a skull with a policeman's hat on. This was a little unnerving, to say the least. *Am I losing my mind here?*

He then changed back to a face again. It was almost like a computer effect, and I couldn't figure out what I was looking at. I got up and walked around, deciding I had worked too much. When I finally went back and sat down, it was still there. *Damn, I wasn't imagining it. What now?* I stared at it and then said out loud, "In the name of Jesus Christ, depart from this place." I made the sign of the cross on myself and repeated it again. "In His name, I tell you to leave here. If you mean harm, leave here."

A hand or something white came up and seemed to wipe across it, but the image was still behind it. I clearly heard the words, "Leave here. Leave here NOW!"

I sat there trying to figure out what was going on. Was I losing my mind or was this really happening? I continued to sit there staring at the image on the wall. Then I heard the words, "Leave here NOW!" again. With that, I stood up and said out loud, "Whoever you are, you don't have to tell me again. I'm gone!" I packed only what I had to and left as quickly as possible, which was literally minutes.

I also seemed to know that I shouldn't tell anyone I was leaving except the renter in the other part of the main house. She looked at me rather strangely as I had just told her, a little while before, that I would be staying a few more days. I then left and went home to my place in Tucson.

★★★

CHAPTER 9: Paranormal Events Intensify

I did not return to the house for some time, only to perform maintenance and upkeep to the home and touch base with my renters. In February of 1992, I moved back into the house. I had been returning monthly to do upkeep and rent portions out. The inability to find steady work and my severely drained finances forced me to return once again. This time, I went on a determined attack to rid my beautiful house of all negative aspects. Lots of religious music resounded through the rooms via my little stereo and cassette tapes. Songs, prayers, and frequent sprinkling of holy water through all the rooms were some of my tactics aimed at clearing the air, so to speak. By Thanksgiving Day, the house felt clean. That is to say, ninety percent of the strange and unexplainable stuff had stopped. Christine came for the holiday and enjoyed her visit. That was a first!

But soon enough it began again.

One night I awoke at three in the morning to the sound of my rocker rocking back and forth vigorously. It kept it up, so I got up, fixed a cup of tea, and just watched it rock. I had two or three smokes and another cup of tea before it stopped. I went back to bed. When I awoke the next morning, I decided that it was probably just a dream. I got up, washed my face, and walked into the living room only to find my teacup and smokes sitting at the little table across from the rocker, and I realized that it had really happened.

Due to an excessive heat wave that we were having, I had to move back into the main section of the house. I had a small air conditioner in the bedroom over there. The renters had moved out again, and no one else had come by to rent the house, so I decided to get more comfortable. My friend of many years, who lived in Arizona, had been worried about me. She also worried that someone was getting into the house at night. She decided that she would bring her big black Doberman Pincer named Lady down and leave her with me for added safety.

I had been around Lady for years, and I loved her dearly. I knew that I didn't have to worry with her in the house with me. She was a huge dog: one-hundred and thirty pounds huge! This amazing dog was trained to protect and totally devoted to me. She went everywhere with me. She loved to ride in the car, take long walks, and even watch TV with me. I was truly in awe the first time she backed up to the sofa and placed her behind and back legs on the cushion with her front paws still on the floor just like a person would sit. What a wonderful companion.

I brought her into my bedroom every night. I rested better for a while knowing she was there to protect me. The first night she stayed with me, I had left a night light on for her, which was not my usual habit. The next morning I found the night light off. I checked the bulb, and it was fine. I checked the plug behind the drapes. When I checked there, I found the plug pulled out of the socket. I knew that Lady would have barked if someone had been

CHAPTER 9: Paranormal Events Intensify

in the room during the night. It was yet another "oh, well" type of moment. Could she have pulled it out with her teeth?

Before very long, I was having problems getting Lady into the room at night. She started getting spooked during the middle of the night. I'd awaken to her barking, then to her poking me with her nose, and then saw her running to the door to get out. Thinking she wanted to go outside, I'd get up, go to the back door, and let her out. She would just wander about and come right back in but not want to return to the bedroom. I would literally have to order her back into the room with me.

Before long, I would find her whimpering and shaking in a ball in the corner of the room. I couldn't get her to stop or even move until I would open the bedroom door. Then, when I did open the door, she would bolt out and refuse to return. I tried leaving the door to the adjoining bathroom open, as well as the door on the opposite wall, which led into the middle bedroom, to allow her more space to roam at night. (I normally kept all the doors leading to other rooms shut and locked during the night. Safety demanded this. However, it was impossible to hear anyone breaking into the house at night due to those twenty-four-inch-thick adobe walls.)

Keeping the bathroom doors open still didn't work. She'd wake me up by banging up against the French doors leading to the dining area. I finally chose to lock both doors leading to my bedroom and open all of the other doors. This gave her the full run of the house at night. It finally worked. Lady was happy with that arrangement.

★★★

There were some manifestations that were not as troublesome as the loud noises and unexplained sightings. I came to see these types of occurrences as more of a game than anything else. I would often find a piece of a child's puzzle on the floor in John's room. It was a large, light blue piece about two by three inches in size. I had never seen it before. It was just lying on the floor one day. I picked it up and laid it on a shelf in the bookshelf area that we had created in an old window area in John's room. I wondered from where it had come.

This was just another unexplainable occurrence, among many. Every now and then, I would find it lying there again, and I'd pick it up and put it on the shelf towards the back. They were deep shelves, and this way I could prove to myself that whoever (or whatever) was moving the piece and I were really playing some kind of game; it couldn't be the wind blowing it off of the shelf or something logically explainable happening.

Another game I played with the home's residents involved a rubber-backed bathmat. I kept it in front of the tub to step on after my bath. Every now and then I'd find it moved and in a different position on the floor. I got so used to these things that they just became part of living there. I'd actually laugh at the humor of their

CHAPTER 9: Paranormal Events Intensify

little ways of letting me know that they were there. The mat was always neatly placed so I'd know it was intentional—not messy like I had kicked it there, or it had been played with by Lady, or anything else accidental.

I considered these as gentle little games perhaps played by the children that others had said that they had seen in the house, such as the little girl that I had spoken of before.

★★★

I spent a lot of time alone in the house. Sometimes, while sitting listening to music, I seemed to hear Frank talking to me. Not audibly, just in my thoughts or my "mind's eye" so to speak. He seemed to be thanking me for telling him about God. His parents were members of that marauding gang that had scourged that area. He robbed, murdered, and committed all kinds of atrocities with no feeling of guilt. He simply knew no other or better way of life.

Since I was abiding in this house together with whatever (or whomever) else, I often spoke out loud in reference to God and played spiritual hymns and such. This was, in part, for my own wellbeing and just in case they were listening, for their benefit also. I prayed for their souls to be at rest and literally told them how much God loves each and every soul, no matter what they've done. I felt that Frank wanted me to know that the absence of the knowledge of God while he was alive was, in some way, a saving grace for him now. If he had known then about the principal of accountability to a higher being for your actions, he would not have been in the position that he was in now; neither damned nor receiving his eternal reward by meeting his Creator. He seemed grateful for my prayers and the music.

I do not claim to understand the reasoning or the meaning to these mental impressions of mine. They may well have been nothing more than that, mental impressions created by an imaginative mind; I really don't know. These things I just seemed to know without knowing how I knew. It made no sense of course, to the logical side of my brain. Then again, it made no sense to me that whenever the door slamming or walking sounds went on too long, I could simply go into the main room of the house and loudly scold, demanding that the nonsense stop right now, and it would! This I experienced many times.

The only time that I may have actually seen a ghostie, and I'm really not sure of that, was one morning when I awoke and opened my eyes to see a young girl. She was standing in the living area of the north wing of the house. My bed faced that area. She appeared to be just looking at me. She had long dark hair parted in the middle and was wearing a sort of crocheted shawl and a long dress. She was maybe five feet tall, at the most. I shut my eyes still drowsy from sleep and suddenly realized what I thought I'd just seen. My eyes flew back open and there was no one there. Was it real or was it a dream? I'm not positive one way or another.

CHAPTER 9: Paranormal Events Intensify

★★★

One weekend, while staying in Tucson with my friend J.C., I told her that I was going to have to go to New Mexico to do some maintenance on the house and asked her if she would like to go with me. She obviously wasn't too thrilled about staying in that house, but she agreed to come along.

We got there midday and unloaded our weekend bags into the north wing, where I stayed whenever I went back at that time, and left to enjoy coffee at the local coffee shop. I called the lady that was taking care of things and let her know that I had arrived in town. We agreed to meet at the house shortly. My friend J.C. had not been there prior to this trip so we took a brief tour through town and then headed back to the house. I sensed her uneasiness but after a while, the beauty of the grounds and good conversation with my other friend seemed to relax her. It was cold that night. We were hungry—time to eat.

We left about nine o'clock and went to a local restaurant and had a good dinner. We decided on the way home to see a little of the local nightlife which was limited in such a small town. As it turned out, a local restaurant had a very good band, and we had a grand 'ole time. About 11:30 or so, we headed back to my house.

The temperature had dropped considerably, as it usually does in the high desert. I was commenting that the little furnace would get the place warm in no time. We hadn't worn any jackets when we left, just some light sweaters, and we were both cold. I put the key in and turned the lock, but the door wouldn't budge. I tried over and over to no avail. We both recalled how I had purposely checked the lock before we left. I had slid the slide-bolt locks into lock position on the other two entrances into that wing of the house and also key locked all three doors. Now there seemed to be no way that we could get in. We were getting so cold that we decided to go rent a room at a local hotel. We'd worry about how to get into the house in the morning.

The next morning, we got a ladder from my garage, climbed up, and looked through the glass window in the transom of the back yard door. I could clearly see why the front door would not open last night. The slide-bolt was in the lock position on that door too! But it didn't make any sense. The slide-bolts took concentrated effort and strength to slide into place. It could not have happened accidentally.

In order to gain entrance to the house, we fashioned a hook out of a wire hanger. I forced open the transom and used the hook to slide the bolt out of the locked position. I had to wedge a broomstick and hook around it to get the leverage needed to get it to move. She pulled on the door at the same time, and we finally got in. It was certainly no easy task.

There was no way, which we could figure out, for someone to lock all three slide-bolts and leave the wing. You had to use one of the doors for an exit! The other two transoms were both bolted and

CHAPTER 9: Paranormal Events Intensify

nailed shut. To open the one we had accessed, I had to force the nail to bend inward, splitting the wooden frame in doing so. It was not loose or tampered with in any way. Whoever locked all three doors so securely would have had to stay in the wing. However, there was no one there when we entered. We immediately grabbed our bags and left. J.C. chose to decline any subsequent offers to accompany me to the house.

★★★

In July of 1993 I had to return to the house once again. I was living and working in Phoenix and received a call informing me that vandals had broken out the large front window in the great room. When I arrived, the glass people had already put in a new window, so I cleaned up the broken glass and added a little more caulking. I replaced my security block on the framing and also remounted the historical information that I kept on the big windows for tourists to see.

My Mexican friend, which I have spoken of, dropped in and invited me to dinner that evening. I agreed. He left and I decided to mop and re-wax the hardwood floors in the great room. They were a real mess in front of the broken window. Someone had been walking in there with wet, muddy shoes. It could have been that the realtor had people coming through or maybe the caretaker visited. Either way, the floors sure needed it. The sun was shining through the multitude of windows. The room was just glowing. In fact, as I walked through checking the house to be sure all was well with her, the beauty overwhelmed me. I stood still for a moment and let it seep into my very soul. *God, how I loved this place!*

I left the house when I was done, went to dinner, and returned in early evening. I watched a little TV, took my bath, and went to bed. Within a half hour, I knew I couldn't sleep in my room that night. The sounds and thick feelings were so intense. I felt my skin begin to crawl. I took my pillow and blanket into the family room to the sofa.

Again, the sounds and peripheral movements intensified. I drifted off to sleep only to awake feeling someone sit down on the sofa. I froze and then felt their breath on my face. Terrified but still trying to prove myself wrong, I took a deep breath and sat up. I put the light on; no one there. I had some tea then went back to the sofa.

I was exhausted and beyond ready for sleep, but I couldn't shake the intensity of the feelings and activity around me. At one point, the presence sat down and touched my hair. I prayed, "Please Lord, let this night be over soon." Finally, dawn mercifully arrived and, with great relief, I walked out the door. Good-bye house.

★★★

On Labor Day weekend of that same year I had to go back to the house to do some yard work and general maintenance. There was lots of junk outside to clean up, and the hedges needed to be cut back. It was a beautiful day, and it felt so good to work in the yard again. I happened to have a vacant guesthouse, so I put my rental signs up.

CHAPTER 9: Paranormal Events Intensify

I decided to stay the weekend and have a nice quiet dinner with my Mexican friend and visit with another dear friend who was not in good health. The evening came, and I had a lovely dinner and good conversation.

But once I returned to the house, the intensity of the activity started again. I kept hearing sounds. *Who's in the great room? No one!* I told myself. *It feels like I'm in a crowd. How ridiculous. There's no one here, just me. I don't think that I want to go through this again tonight. I feel hostile feelings in here again. To hell with bravery, I'm tired. I'm going to go to a motel.*

It's so strange how the whole atmosphere changed in the house at night. I came back and cleaned up my tools and other belongings and left the following day. That was the third or fourth time I had felt that I couldn't stay in the house. Each time that it happened, it was after I had been away for a while or just before I was to leave. It seemed the ghosties would get upset if I left and also when I would return. Like children, they didn't like changes. I guess we adults are that way to some extent as well.

★★★

It became all too apparent to me that I needed to find a way to sell the house to someone who would love her and treasure her, eccentricities and all, as I had. The intensity of the hostile feelings in the home when I visited prohibited me from staying long, and they were both emotionally and physically draining. I had also found a life somewhere else, and I simply could not keep up with all of the maintenance of the property from so far away. I longed for her to have her place in history and to be celebrated accordingly. It was time to begin the long good-bye.

CHAPTER 10

Saying Goodbye

"I love her, but I'm so alone."

As my thoughts returned to the reason I had chosen the beautiful area of Deming and subsequently purchased the Golden House, I considered how much I, and my children alike, really loved the American West.

My family was my number one priority, so I chose Deming as a safe "home base" of sorts from which they could launch into their adult lives. Becoming an adult is, at best, a confusing and difficult time in life. My job, I felt, was like that of a mother bird. My desire was to help them become adults—self-sufficient and fully able to exist without me. One by one, the time for each to be gently pushed out of the nest came; it was time to stand on their own two feet and realize that they could! These were my God-given responsibilities, by virtue of their births. If I did this job well, they would decide to keep me in their lives out of choice, not necessity.

I thought back to the day my husband and I had explored Deming in the hopes of finding an investment property. My, how things had changed since then.

★★★

Despite the many hours toiling to bring the house to her former glory, the work to get this U.S. Customs House declared a federal, state, and national historic site and gaining her entry into the National Registry of Historic Places, and simply my love for the home, it was time to let her go. I felt like I had been there forever, and I was growing weary of the loneliness and isolation. I loved her, but I was so alone.

The upkeep was horrendous and very costly. My funds were running out. According to my estimates, we put more than $50,000 into the restoration of the home. I wanted to be out from under the burden of the upkeep and financial strain of the home, but I also wanted her to be in good hands.

★★★

At one time, a Catholic nun came to town, and I thought for a while that maybe her order would have use for the house as a

Chapter 10: Saying Goodbye

convent. I prayed a lot about it, and I thought this might be my answer to prayer. Unfortunately, I could figure no way to donate it to them. I was deeply in debt myself from all of the upkeep involved in the property. It would have been a blessing to me to sell or donate the property and be out from under the burden of her care. But after a while, I realized that this was not to be.

A couple from England came to see the house one day. The husband ran a school with a religious foundation. I again began to hope that this might be the path for which I was praying. However, this too went by the wayside. Their offer was simply not enough. I knew that I just had to hang on until the future of that dear old place fell into view. Save her, I must. This I knew without the slightest doubt.

I began to wonder if the home would be of any interest to the U.S. Customs Department as a museum of sorts. I wrote a letter to Customs in October of 1993 to plead with them to consider buying the house. The written response I received was disheartening. They did not seem to understand how important the home and the town of Deming were to U.S. History. I felt as if I had hit a brick wall, but I kept working away at getting the property sold. I even placed a statue of St. Joseph in the yard for good luck.

In an unexpected turn of events in March of 1994, I received word that the city of Deming would be purchasing the home to be used as a museum, utilizing funds from the state of New Mexico. The wonderful part of this transition was that I didn't have to worry about any future residents and what they would have to endure. The ghosties could be alone at night and not bothering anyone else. I wouldn't be "inflicting" the place on any unsuspecting buyers. My heart was glad—my journey seemed to finally be coming to an end.

After the governor of New Mexico signed the vote to buy the property, the sale was official in April 1994. The National Trust granted funds to the state who, via grant, added it to the museums of New Mexico. I did endure some problems with having paperwork delayed, but eventually the Golden House was in the very capable hands of the city of Deming. The lady at the museum across the street assured me that she would do everything she could to keep her going.

I got to work preparing the house for my departure. Everything in the house was sold at a steep discount through an ad in the paper. In a matter of only two days, the house was completely cleaned out! I joke that they robbed me blind, but in truth I just wanted a fresh start. I took only my clothes and some stained glass, paid off all my bills, and started a new chapter in my life. It had been the experience of a lifetime, but one that I would not want to repeat.

In the moments when I was tempted to give up or run away from the burden of the home and the terror of some of the experiences I had, I kept the following poem in mind:

Don't Quit

When things go wrong, as they sometimes will,
When the road you're trudging seems all uphill,
When the funds are low and the debts are high,
And you want to smile, but you have to sigh,
When care is pressing you down a bit—
Rest if you must, but don't you quit.

Life is queer with its twists and turns,
As every one of us sometimes learns,
And many a fellow turns about
When he might have won had he stuck it out.
Don't give up though the pace seems slow—
You may succeed with another blow.

Often the goal is nearer than
It seems to a faint and faltering man;
Often the struggler has given up
When he might have captured the victor's cup;
And he learned too late when the night came down,
How close he was to the golden crown.

Success is failure turned inside out—
The silver tint in the clouds of doubt,
And you never can tell how close you are,
It might be near when it seems afar;
So stick to the fight when you're hardest hit -
It's when things seem worst that you must not quit.

—Unknown

★★★

In the days after the sale of the property, I had very mixed emotions. In some ways, I felt great relief in having passed the torch, so to speak. I put my feelings for her to rest with self-assurances. She was no longer mine to care for. Those that had her now would treasure her as I and so many others had.

I drove down to see her recently, before her opening day as a museum. She's changed a great deal, but she still stands and I know all within are ready to put their best foot forward. We, the American people (for it is our tax dollars that purchased her via public monies in grant form), do put our trust in those responsible for her care and upkeep. Protect her. Cherish her. Do her no harm.

Do not view her as just a big old house. She is an American treasure. So states the National Trust, the State of New Mexico, and the Federal Treasury Department. Respect is deserved—she's earned it in sheltering so many for so long.

To all the readers of this story, I encourage you, if you're down that way, to stop in and see her. Say "hello" for me if you do. The Golden House is located just two blocks off the interstate near the center of town. If you like art as well as history, stop in the local art council showroom and view the work of such talented artists as Margot and Paul Hoylen, Dorothy Tuma, Loretta Cain, Paulie White, Joan Ackert and Johnnie Clarey. See drawings by John Trowbridge, (Seaman Field's great-grandson). You will also find photographs by Dallas Johnson, husband of one of the most brilliant and talented women I've ever met. These are just a few names, among so many. Scores of fine artists, of all mediums, abound in this area.

All of the places, people, and things which I have spoken of await you. Maybe even a light touch to your hair, a breath on the back of your neck or possibly a touch on your arm. When you turn to see who is there (and no one is), say "hello" for me too.

There are still more stories to tell, but I think I'll let you discover them for yourself. I hope you've enjoyed my story—a story that had to be told.

The End

EPILOGUE

No Better Place to Call Home

"It was fun to see people from other nations stop in and ask about the 'Real American West' and then watch their eyes light up when you assured them, 'You're here!'"

I hope that my love for the southwest, and New Mexico area in particular, have come through in this book. In choosing this region as a location for my family to call home, my priority was often directed toward the goal of assuring each of my children the security of a home base—a place to finish high school and decide which direction to go in their lives. As I explained in the last chapter, I wanted a good home base from which they could launch into adulthood.

Though my relocation to New Mexico and the greater southwest area began as a search for an investment opportunity and a fresh start for my husband and me, that first little trip to Deming was a turning point in my life in so many other ways. I couldn't possibly have fathomed the influence that the beautiful art, history, and geography of the New Mexico would have on my soul. As I grew to know the region and the people, I simply fell in love. I invite you to join me on a virtual tour of the region in the next few pages. Grab a cup of coffee, put your feet up, and imagine the discoveries that await you in this captivating area of the United States. Perhaps you will be moved to explore for yourself one day.

★★★

New Mexico, where the property in this story exists, is a fascinating place. Points of interest lie in every direction. The Florida, Mountains (pronounced Floor-ee-da), are fifteen minutes from the house. So named for the abundant display of wild poppies, the rugged mountains also sport wild Persian Ibex, released into the mountains in 1970 by the New Mexico Department of Fish and Game. Rock Hound State Park, located just to the north, is well known for its abundance of semi-precious stones. This is also considered the fabled residence of the famous Indian leader, Victorio, at various times. There are tales of a hidden treasure. An army payroll consisting of a chest full of gold was robbed from a stage coach and hidden in those mountains. It was never found and is still searched for right up to the time of this writing.

The Mimbres Indians occupied the entire area from about 950 to 1200 A.D. Known for their amazing artistic talents, they left behind a profound story via their pottery. It is superior in design and is abundant in that region. I saw pictures of a cave, with Apache Kachinas standing eight to ten feet tall, painted on walls tinted in soft blue and pink. They seemed to be coming right out of the walls at you. I became acquainted with a local man who had an amazing collection of Mimbreno artifacts. He allowed them to be viewed in the Gallery during the celebrations held there with the Customs Department. He told me that he had taken these photos in a cave in the Floridas. I never got a chance to go see the paintings in person, much to my regret.

Heading further south lies Columbus, New Mexico, the only spot in our continental United States that was ever invaded by a foreign force. Pancho Villa's infamous raid took place there in 1916. Our nation's first military use of air power was a result of that raid and was led by the Army Signal Corps First Aero Squadron out of Fort Sam Houston, Texas. Columbus is a tiny border town that's beginning to grow. A large new port of entry building sits about three miles past Columbus, on the actual American border, south of town. Nearby is a new Aerostat facility which is used by law enforcement for aerial surveillance. It was officially dedicated to that region on December 3, 1988. We helped host that event at the house.

The Mexican town of Palomas is just across the border from Columbus, about thirty miles from the house. It is as quaint of a town as one could wish to visit. On Saturday afternoons, many Mexican and Indian vendors from farther south into Mexico would come up to Palomas. Their costumes were so colorful and interesting. Mariachi bands played here and there throughout the day. A wonderful bakery offered delicious, fresh and unusual baked goodies. Great buys were to be found on leather goods, ceramics, jewelry, and more. It was a truly fun and interesting way to spend and afternoon.

To the east, about fifty or sixty miles, lies Las Cruces, New Mexico. Just before reaching Las Cruces on Interstate 10 is a sign which reads, "Historic Mesilla—turn right." About four miles down that road is one of my very favorite places. A very old town square and shops full of treasures, old and new. Billy the Kid is said to have been held on trial in a corner building when he escaped and fled justice. Just across the street is a Mexican restaurant, the La Posta, which was an old stage stop. In the square is a very old Catholic church and a wonderful restaurant called the Double Eagle. This restaurant is truly fine dining in an old Spanish villa. It even features a verified picture of a ghostly visitor, caught by the camera's eye and hung on the wall.

Elegant antique furnishings of deep velvets and gold brocades adorn the outer rooms. A matador's costume encased in glass is another treasure found within. In the middle of the villa is an atrium with glass top tables and white wicker chairs, crystal goblets for water and lush foliage including bougainvillea and hanging ivy. Each room is a collector's delight. Additional features of this beautiful Spanish oasis include a polished wood bar that seems to be a mile long and a ballroom with black and white tile. At one end of the ballroom are French doors leading out to a wide veranda. Positioned halfway up one wall is a balcony designed to house a band, and on the opposite wall hangs a huge picture of one of the late Mexican emperors. The La Posta also has an aviary with various types of parrots and other birds including one who whistles at the ladies. I think he called me "Babe" when I crossed paths with him.

There are many other unique establishments in the Mesilla square. One such place is a neat little chocolate shop where you can buy a postcard made out of chocolate. You can also purchase or a rose, a basket or other trinket, all made out of chocolate: either dark or white. Several shops are filled with antiques and others sell import items from various countries. There is even a park in the square with an old bandstand. I visited Mesilla one day just meandering. What a great afternoon!

Heading north from the house, your first stop is Fort Cummings. This old military outpost sits about ten miles northeast of the house. Some of its original walls still stand. Many of the foundations and sections of the structures are still intact. Your emotions and thoughts can't help but go out to those soldiers and Indian people, who struggled so, on this very spot. Graves of soldiers killed by Apaches lie scattered across the desert floor. This is a place of great sorrow where many lost their lives. The way leading into and out of that fort became so dangerous, and the trail so bloody, that the government finally closed and abandoned the place in the mid 1800's.

Next stop will be the City of Rocks. A surreal place of huge rocks, jutting out of the desert floor and resembling a city you might expect to see on another planet. The elements have carved the rocks into strange shapes and configurations. Some of which are hollow and make weird sounds when the dry southwestern wind blows full and strong. Geologists come from all over the world to hear this wonderful phenomenon while gazing at the result of Mother Nature's artistic display.

Driving north father yet, you reach Silver City. This beautiful town, nestled among the pines, boasts some great western history, wonderful art and a fine university. A very talented artist named Sharon Evans lives there. She introduced me to the beauty of this area via her paintings. We became really good friends over the years.

Over in the Gila Wilderness you will find magnificent Indian ruins and abundant wildlife of all types. This is an area of natural beauty that equals any that I've seen. Piños Altos is an old gold mining community where the Hearst family made their fortune, I am told. You will also find an old 1800's saloon that features real furnishings from that era as well as some very good food. An opera house from the same time period adjoins the saloon. Every time I went there, I always felt that at any minute, Marilyn Monroe was going to sashay out onto that little stage and begin to sing. The little balconies would then fill up with the true western crowd of miners, cowboys and slick gamblin' men, all there to see the show. The emotional aura was always thick in that room with all the sounds of those wild, whiskey drinking, hard time old days. The opera house features a collection of Mimbres pottery and Indian artifacts that covers an entire wall.

What a fantastic place! I've been told that they're re-opening the old mines there again. It seems that the price of gold these days makes it worthwhile to glean the leftovers from those old dusty mines. Amidst all of this western history and culture lies Lake Roberts offering great fishing with boats and little cabins to rent.

Silver City has a small airport. Deming also has an airport, but it is anything but small. The airport there is an old WWII airbase which has been converted to a regional commuter stop.

Heading west, you will find Lordsburg, New Mexico (an old railroad town), the Chiricahua Mountains, Fort Bowie and ghost towns left from frontier days gone by. Continuing west you'll come to Bisbee, Arizona, with the Copper Queen Hotel of John Wayne fame and a mining area famous for its turquoise. Then it's onto the San Carlos Apache Indian Reservation and Tombstone, another infamous western town, with the O.K. Corral.

During my years in this area, I often visited these places I have just described to you, with my husband, my children, several guests and friends. I went to several of these areas quite often, sometimes to share them with others and sometimes to create some private time with my children.

When our art gallery, bed and art accommodations, cabinetry and stained glass shop, and gift shop was opened, I delighted in relating the many wonderful places that residents and tourists alike could visit in surrounding areas.

The visitor sign in book I kept is a treasured reminder of that time in my life. It has names of people from all over this great nation and many from the rest of the world. They put their comments down and reading these remarks initiate memory trips that I can take every now and then. I remember that nice couple from New Zealand and that lovely lady from Spain. It was fun to see people from other nations stop in and ask about the "Real American West" and then watch their eyes light up when you assured them, "You're here!"

Seaman Field and His Wife

Dedication Ceremony April 22, 1989

Back of house

Backyard Flower Bed

Main room

Kitchen with Pantry Door Open (front left)

Main Room

View from Living Room into Kitchen

Master Bedroom and Site of the Recurring Bloodstains

APPENDIX

Recorded Property Deeds

MARCH 17, 1842: TREATY TO RELOCATE WYANDOTTE FLOAT NO. 9

PROCLAIMED ON OCTOBER 5, 1842. REAFFIRMED UNDER TREATY OF JANUARY 31, 1855. PROCLAIMED MARCH 12, 1855.

Recorded at U.S. Land Office, Mesilla, NM, February 16, 1881. Recorded by H.K. Pickney for Irwin P. Long. Mr. Pickney presenting Power-of-Attorney for Mr. Long.

Geo. D. Bowman-Register

General of New Mexico at Santa Fe. 640 acres situated in T.23 S. Range 9 W.N.M.M. Filed with Surveyor

The above treaty information is part of what I, the author, have researched. I have come to believe, in agreement with other persons who joined in the information hunt, that this is the first legal documentation of American ownership of the property on Silver Street; legally recorded in deed form in books registering transactions for obvious reasons. This does not reflect the U.S. Customs book of record which shows tariff collections, etc. as early as 1848 at this outpost and port of entry. The fact that the land was given by treaty to Mr. Long in 1842 asserts that our government was occupying this area and was able to grant it in treaty at that time to Mr. Long. The Gadsden Purchase was not official until 1853. Other purchase agreements were being negotiated for quite some time prior to the final agreement of 1853.

For those of you interested, I offer the following chain of ownership for this property. If you look closely, you'll discover a great deal about that historical era.

DEEDS OF LOTS 1 THRU 5 - BLOCK 18 OF DEMING NM OR ANY PART OF ANY PARCEL CONTAINING THESE LOTS. (These being the lots on which the Golden House property is located)

LOTS 1 & 2

FEBRUARY 25, 1881

LONG TO A.A. ROBINSON

MISSOURI

APPENDIX: Recorded Property Deeds 123

LOTS 3 & 4

NOVEMBER 22, 1882

ROBINSON TO DRUNEGAL

KANSAS

LOTS 1 & 2

DECEMBER 8, 1882

ROBINSON TO OETTINGER

KANSAS

(LOTS NOT DEFINED) .57 AND .27 ACRES SOLD.

NOVEMBER 2, 1883

ROBINSON TO EDWARD MILLER

KANSAS

LOTS 5 & 6

DECEMBER 24, 1883

WILDER TO A. FROST AND J. STROMBERG

KANSAS

LOT 4

JANUARY 1884

DRONEGAL TO CARRIE MOSHER [HUGHES]

ARIZONA

LOT 3

APRIL 26, 1884

DRUNEGAL TO Wm JONES

ARIZONA

JUNE 28, 1884

JONES TO DANE (For mortgage security only - paid off April 6, 1885)

LOT 3

MARCH 5, 1885

Wm JONES TO FRANK THURMOND (QUIT CLAIM)

NEW MEXICO

APPENDIX: Recorded Property Deeds

LOT 3

MARCH 25, 1885

THURMOND TO ROBERT S. FIELD (QUIT CLAIM)

NEW MEXICO

LOT 4   [RECORDED ON OCTOBER 17, 1887]

JUNE 12, 1887

CARRIE MOSHER [HUGHES] TO SEAMAN FIELD

CALIFORNIA

*(Carrie sold same lot to Gardiner/Gillies on February 4, 1889)

LOT 3

FEBRUARY 1, 1888

R.S. FIELD TO SEAMAN FIELD

NEW MEXICO

LOTS 5 & 6

AUGUST 28, 1888

JOHN STROMBERG TO L.C. BOURK

COLORADO (½ UNDIVIDED INTEREST)

LOTS 1 & 2

MARCH 7, 1889

OETTINGER TO B.Y. McKEYES/WASHINGTON

MEXICO CITY

U.S. CONSULATE GENERAL - REPUBLIC OF MEXICO

LOTS 5 & 6

MARCH 25, 1889

AARON FROST TO SEAMAN FIELD

SAN DIEGO, CA (½ UNDIVIDED INTEREST)

LOTS 5 & 6

APRIL; 16, 1889

BOURK TO SEAMAN FIELD

COLORADO (½ UNDIVIDED INTEREST)

APPENDIX: Recorded Property Deeds

LOTS 1 & 2

MAY 1, 1889

WASHINGTON TO McKEYES

NEW MEXICO (½ UNDIVIDED INTEREST)

LOTS 1 THRU 20

MAY 2, 1889

G. WORMSER TO OLD & NEW MEXICO IMPROVEMENT CO.

LOTS 1 & 2

AUGUST 13, 1892

McKEYES TO CHARLES SCOLFIELD

NEW MEXICO (½ UNDIVIDED INTEREST)

LOTS 1 & 2

AUGUST 16, 1892

SCOLFIELD TO SEAMAN FIELD

NEW MEXICO (½ UNDIVIDED INTEREST)

LOTS 1 & 2

NOVEMBER 10, 1892

McKEYES TO SEAMAN FIELD

NEW MEXICO (½ UNDIVIDED INTEREST)

www.ingramcontent.com/pod-product-compliance
Lightning Source LLC
Chambersburg PA
CBHW070053120526
44588CB00033B/1415